To Irene

Happy X Mas 85

From

Peter.

THE POET'S CIRCUITS

PADRAIC COLUM

The Poet's Circuits

COLLECTED POEMS OF IRELAND

WITH A PREFACE BY
BENEDICT KIELY

THE DOLMEN PRESS

THE POET'S CIRCUITS is printed in the Republic of Ireland
by O'Brien Promotions Limited for the publishers,
The Dolmen Press, Mountrath, Portlaoise, Ireland.

General Distributors in North America: Humaities Press Inc.,
171 First Avenue, Atlantic Highlands, New Jersey 07716, U.S.A.

This edition first published in 1981, the centenary year of Padraic
Colum's birth. It reproduces, with amendments, the typesetting of the
1960 edition, by permission of the Oxford University Press. The Preface
by Benedict Kiely was written for this edition which is published in
association with the Padraic Colum Centenary National Committee.
Reprinted 1985.

The Dolmen Press receives finacial assistance from
The Arts Council, An Comhairle Ealaíon, Ireland.

The cover reproduces an illustration by Jack B. Yeats to 'She Moved
Through the Fair' originally printed in *A Broadside*, 1912, by permission
of Miss Anne Yeats and The Cuala Press Limited.

British Library in Publication Data
    Colum, Padraic
        The poet's circuits.—Centenary ed.
        I. Title
        821'.912   RP6005.038

    ISBN 0 85105 390 4

Contents

Preface

The poet in the candle-light and with his head up to the rafters said that the birds that sing best in the woods are reared with breasts to the clay; and that close to the ground were reared the wings with the widest sway. It is a simpler, less overpowering way of expressing what W.B. Yeats was up to when he said that he and John Synge and Augusta Gregory thought that all that they did, said or sang must come from contact with the soil, that, from that contact everything Antaeus-like grew strong; and, with his passion for exclusiveness, that he and Synge and Lady Gregory, alone in modern times has brought everything down to that sole test again'.

Antaeus is too gigantically clumsy for the context; and he suffered badly when his feet were off the ground; and a gossip in Gort once said to Philip Rooney that Lady Gregory never entered a shop in Gort but sat in her conveyance and sent the coachman in with the passbook. Padraic Colum, in all truth, may like the lapwing have gone closer to the ground and the land and been close to the people who actually worked on it; and the images of the poet he invokes for us are as friendly as the hearthlight.

There is the basket-maker, a nameless man, an itinerant, one of the many travelling people whom, in his boyhood, Colum saw on the roads of an Ireland that has now almost vanished from the memory of man. His hands were as supple as the rods he bended. Those willow rods shone like amber. He used no tools but his hands and a knife that he had carried since his apprenticeship, and that brought with it all the memories of his youth. Carefully he wove rod over rod, no gap between the ridges; and knew that the work he left behind him as he went would be marked by no craftsman's name; be nothing more than common household goods. The basket-maker has no name', he said.

Yet he knew that in Kerry glens the weavers' bundles were carried in creels that he had made; and to the young poet, Colum, he showed a Claddagh ring that an old woman had given him in payment for baskets that were a benefit to carry her fish to Galway. So he went his way, leaving the young poet with the withied shape his hands had made; and with an image and an ideal:

> I watched him go, his stock-in-trade upon him.
> I travel Ireland's length and breadth,' he said.
> There was dominion in the way he said it,
> And in his even way towards other roofs,
> A basket-maker, an itinerant.

An Irish poet of our own time has found images of his art in watching a thatcher at work on the loughshore, or in watching his father digging in a garden: the pen's my spade, I'll dig with that.

Through a street in which Padraic once lived there used to walk, calling his wares, a man selling, of all things, combs of honey. It is not a sight that we are liable to see today; and the carbon monoxide on our streets would rob the Hybla bees and leave them honeyless. But long ago that man went by, on his head a wide dish, holding dark and golden lumps of honey. The people in that street must have distrusted the bees or the dark comb in which a living sting might, for the careless eater, still linger. For no one ever bought, no one ever paid a penny for a single comb of sweetness:

> Yet you went, a man contented
> As though you had a king to call on
> Who would take you to his parlour,
> And buy all you stock of honey.
> On you went, and in a sounding
> Voice, just like the bell of evening,
> Told us of the goods you carried,

Told us of the dark and golden
Treasure dripping on your wide dish.

You went by, and no one named you.

On another street he once saw a captive fox, leashed and
led like other canines, but sidling with all the terror a creature
of the wild might feel at the trampling of men and the rearing
of horses. The machine had not yet taken over. The poet
thought of the ancient customs of Irrus where people left out
mittens for foxes, where, for luck, foxes were invited to
christenings. Did a fox ever turn up at the font? Where foxes
were named as gossips for boys and girls. Magic as old as
Egypt. He thought that if an Irrus boy whom he had once
known had been present on that street he would have told his
gossip that a human being had heart for him, would have
found some way to bring:

His rainy hills around him, the soft grass,
Darkness of ragged hedges, and his earth
The black, damp earth under the roots of trees.

Images of the poet out of a lost time and in an uncompre-
hending world; and they may stand valid for our time or as
long as the earth is allowed to survive. A contemporary
American poet found shattering matter for thought when he
saw that some fond and bitter man had scrawled in terrible
irony on the dirty wall of a subway station: The woods of
Arcady are dead'. And Yeats had prayed that his daughter's
bridgroom would bring her to a house, where all's accus-
tomed, ceremonious'. That house, or its first cousin, Padraic
Colum saw in his novel, *Castle Conquer,* in the house of
Owen Paralon, and here in the Wordsworthian prelude to
The Poet's Circuits.

Owen Paralon recalled, for the young boy who was to be
a poet, a house that once had more life between its walls than

it or any other house in the neighbourhood would ever know again: on one bench a carter mending harness, there a woman carding wool or a girl spinning yarn and, where the light was best, a thresher binding his flail with eelskin; and, around the hearth, the poet and the scholar, the pilgrim and the story-teller. In one corner by the hearth a sack of leaves or heather tops for the homeless wanderer; and the woman of the house presiding over all, taking from the oven the high brown bread baked from wheat from the bottom field, ground in the mill close-by, to serve as supper for the labourers with mugs of new milk and fresh-churned butter, and a goose-egg beside each platter.

> A lively house indeed', a neighbour said.
> I mind the songs, I mind the discourse in it.
> But who'll have memory of them when we're gone.'

Something is lost, Owen Paralon said, in every change that comes. Something may also be gained. But for that, and the world being the way it is, we have to wait and see: and hope.

BENEDICT KIELY

July 1981

Foreword

THE Poet's Circuits! In medieval Ireland a poet from time to time crossed the boundary of the canton he had residence in and went through other cantons, giving recitals, meeting distinguished members of his guild, looking in on bardic schools, and closing with return to residence, bearing proper fees. We know of one poet, Cuirithir, whose emotional history came out of a circuit he made. Perhaps the poet who in disgust made a quatrain on the lord who paid him with a cow instead of with the steed he expected has recorded an experience on a circuit. And I like to think that the poem in which the Lady of Moyne is so humorously consoled for the loss of her pet goose was composed by a circuit-making poet.* The title of the collection, then, has to do with a poet who, professionally and as one with a function, makes his.

My early training as a writer was in the theatre, and so when, after juvenilia, I began to write publishable verse, what I produced took the form of dramatic lyrics, poems arising out of character and situations—'A Drover', 'A Poor Scholar', 'An Old Woman of the Roads'. (But I could claim that in doing this I followed a traditional bent in Irish poetry: in the tenth century there are poems attributed to Columcille, to Grainne, to Eve even, poems that project character and situation.*) Dramatic lyrics imply succession: if this character and this situation are projected, why not other characters and other situations? And so, the theatre being back of me, it was inevitable that I should continue the writing of dramatic lyrics. After some decades of such writing I found I had enough poems of a particular kind to make a representative showing of persons and situations in an Irish countryside.

In so far as they have a succession, continuity, in so far as they are representative of a countryside, these poems of men and

* See G. Murphy, *Early Irish Lyrics* (Oxford University Press, London, 1956).

xi

women make a sequence, or, to leave aside a word that has become technical, a saga. It is as a saga and not as separate pieces that they should be presented. They come under traditional influences: many of the personae are engaged in traditional occupations; some of the poems are reconstructions of traditional songs and are fitted to traditional music; others are translations of pieces that have traditional existence in Gaelic.

When I came to look for a way of arranging them, a traditional way, I felt, would avail me best. And so the medieval circuit came into my mind. It lapsed before it came to our time, but to many Irish poets the poetic circuit is still a valid conception. And it appealed personally, not only because it gives movement and prospect of observing characters, but because it assumes that the poet has a function, an obligation, a dedication, a definable territory to make his circuit through. The circuits the poet would make would be territorial, but they would also be through areas of occupations and interests.

Where begin? Here is the field with its primal employments and alongside it the road with its goings and comings from and to market and fair. A poet making circuits through areas of occupations and interests might well begin there. However, I relegated this arrangement to second place when I turned into the house. The traditional has its centre there. By the turf fire on the hearthstone, stories, poetry, local history were repeated; around it occurred the exchanges of the *ceilidhe* which had kept pointed discourse alive in Ireland; and the hearth was the centre of such learning as was, at a certain period, obtainable by the people.

The circuits begin in the house and with the entrance of traditional music and song, and then go to the field and the road alongside it. What is accessible from medieval life is encountered in the third circuit. The last circuit is not as plain as the others. The culture of the cottage has decayed. But as the two who remembered it turn away they find that the great house that for so long dominated the cottage has also gone into decay. Back further it is the Norman castle; it is the Irish Cashel; it is the bronze-age Dún; it is the unremembered cromlech. Between the sights are snatches that refer to orders that were once established—a Jacobite lament, a seventeenth-century vision of restoration, a song of the times before the war that Cromwell ended; a lament that comes out of an English raid across a border. The poem that closes the circuit and ends the collection speaks of historical changes as coming out of the imagination that is destined to pass into other moods.

Those who sat at the hearth with me and supplied the figures and the language that went into my imagination are gone; the poets whom I talked to and whose instruction I profited by are now few in number. One to whom I dedicated a section of these poems is no longer here. But the dedication that was to the living —how living in everything that belonged to poetry!—stays.

MARY CATHERINE MAGUIRE COLUM

They come to it and take
Their cupfuls and their palmfuls out of it,
The well that's marked for use and gossiping.

Who know
Whence come the waters? Through what passages
Beneath? From what high tors
Where forests are? Forests dripping rain,
Branches pouring to the ground, trunk, bark, roots
Letting their streamlets down? Through the earth's dark
The water flows and finds a secret hollow.
Stones are around it and a thorn bush
And so the well is made familiar,
Marked, used, resorted to day after day.

No users, gossipers, the half-moon above!
Come to the well, my own, my bright-haired one,
And let me hear
The rapture of your voice with some great line
Of verse your memory holds, the while your look
Ecstatic is your spirit in your face,
And maybe in a depth below the depth
Touched by a pail, something desired will stir.

P. C.

Fore-piece

I

FROM where the solitary crow, the grey,
Infamous in our sagas, fluttered over
The flatness of the bog, to where familiar
Crows gathered in the trees beside a house,
He drove me: there were miles of rutted road.

It was the Easter of my twentieth year,
And Easter was betokened: half-grown lambs
Beside their mothers in a rocky field;
Black cattle making tracks
Between the golden bushes of the whins;
The crops enclosed with hedges, and the bog
Rough with the heather that had shade of bloom.

As in Fenian stories
Some man unheard of forcefully comes in,
And by demands he makes turns things around
And changes someone's history, he came
Into my days that were unlike the heroes',
And his demand was only that I take
His hospitality. So here I was
Mounted beside him on his outside car
With mare between the shafts—Owen Paralon.

Not only in his advent was he like
The man in Fenian stories, but in the way
His speech became narration as we went
Between the hedgerows, for he told about
The fair of Ballinasloe, the three-day fair

Where one could prove oneself an Irishman
By quickness in the judgement of a horse.
It would be just as blundering, he averred,
For one like him to show misjudgement there,
As for one not to know the dance's figure
In house where people gathered on Shrove Night,
And had to place himself behind the door
For shame of ignorance; his story was of horses
Fed on choice oats and led around by owners,
And eyed by men who knew in lift of head
A horse's spirit, and his paces in
The way he lifted hooves upon the street.
And while he spoke of this, the big-boned mare
Went steadily and well.

                              Remembrance came to me:
My father's and my mother's forefathers
Lived where such fields
With crops and cattle brought the year around,
But we were born, myself and other children,
In borough where my father held an office,
And though the distance
To these old places were in tens of miles,
It meant for us, the children, ruggedness,
Strange faces and cramped houses, generations
One had not lived with, who instructed us
In other ways, whose kindness was from far.
And once when I had come to Confirmation,
And had received the seven ghostly gifts,
Among them being the Gift of Understanding,
I found myself in one of these thatched houses.
The only inmates, children welcomed me:
They made me one of that mysterious household
That children own; they even showed me
The footstep in the ash that was Saint Brighid's.

And now we came to where upon the trees
Crows with all harshness served discordant broods,
And here was my host's house, Owen Paralon's.
The walls were thick, as though some castle builder
Had stooped to raise a house that would have only
Bedrooms and attic over living room;
A farmer's house with grunting of the pigs,
And geese's gabble coming from the yard.
A comely woman stood upon the doorstep
To welcome me—the woman of the house.

The timber that the bog had long preserved
Blazed on the hearth; the benches, table,
Meal-chest and dresser, showed a craftsman's choice
Of oak or ash or elm, and fit design.
And there was that that gave largesse to all:
Above a wild duck with a glistening neck,
And brown dead hare, there shone a silver cup.

And who was I that with such great elation
Was brought into this house? One without mark,
And solitary, since I had been removed
From places I had known, one whose nearest
Were dead or scattered, one who had such thoughts
As those who have no prospects entertain—
Inconsequential, unfulfilling, void.
As profitless in friendship as in wage
My means of living; the solitariness
Was occupying mind, for I had found
A refuge in repository of books
Of dream and speculation, books that made
The world spectral for me, that I read
Fondly. Then this man came
And prayed that I would come to him some time.

And in the promise that I made to him
What challenge was there? I lived with reveries,
Soliloquies, and guesses that detained me,
And from these turning was to lose my way.
The promise that I gave went with resolve.

'A great man of his word', he said of me,
When we had eaten, and 'word' and 'man'
Took on a meaning over the hearthstone,
As though no one who had not pledged himself
Had title to be there. Johanna showed
That she already had good thought of me.

The pair were married half a lifetime; they
Had daughter only; she was gone from them,
And was a nun professed.

                    And why had he
Sought me and brought me to this seat beside
His hearth? Because as some day brings
A memory of a day when one had joy
And all things had a glow, he had bethought
Of one he met in some bright company
He was not used to, and that never again
He entered, or saw her ever again,
And then a memory had taken him,
And he had come to see one of her rearing,
(So chance was present in this happening!)
And having come, drew out of me a pledge.
(Yes, chance! But will had seconded the chance!)
And here was I who for this evening felt
A hostage in a land of golden whin,
Black cattle and the bog with heather rough.

4

He was a six-foot man, Owen Paralon,
But that good size
Was but a frame for him; his was a face
So clear of line a sculptor might have set it
Above the carved door of an oratory
With faces of the princes and the craftsmen
Whom he had known, faces that ne'er looked on
Olympian games nor consular processions,
But have proportion due to deed and thought.
The rugged brows
Above the deep-set eyes put him before
The easy-going; between brow and lip
The nose was straightly chiselled, and the mouth
Ready for speech, ready for judgements,
And there was humour in its changing line:
Indeed his face
Was like the land the light is quick upon
And changes from one instant to another.

Another evening when he sat with neighbours
To talk of farming matters, I was by
Where she, the woman of the house, used needle,
The wide spread of the quilt upon her knees,
The lamp, not candles, burning; there I heard
Talk of new grass and watched her fingers ply.

Night after night
The fire burned down in ashes, holding sparks
To be rekindled and to glow and fade
All through the day. I watched her draw the needle
Back to her shoulder, then put stitches through
The patch of red or black that she was quilting.
My gaze was held by these repeated motions.
And at the table Owen Paralon
And his three neighbours plotted grass in fields.

I sat where there was custom—
Where men were mindful of the coming grass,
And where upon her knees a quilt was growing
A homely grandeur, patched with red and black.
The bog-deal blazed:
I had no custom, and I lived at random:
I would go back to what was, would be mine—
Long walks at night about the streets of a town
Where no one knew me, and to musings over
Books that were musings of unplanted men.

And now Owen Paralon and his three neighbours
Came to the hearth: the silver cup was brought him,
And whiskey for each man of us was poured
Out of a jar; we drank with ceremony:
An old-time leader had drunk out of it.

'The quilt will be a cover for you, son,
When you come back,' Johanna said to me.
The pause she made, the needle at her shoulder
Was like a turn in verse. Then I saw more:
The red and black were made in tufted patches:
She raised the patch she would put needle through
With paper scraps were in a basket by her.
I lifted up
A scrap of paper, and saw lines upon it
Made by a quill, and saw they were in Latin,
And knew them Virgil's by their poetry
Although they were about the bulls and cows,
Their mating and the cleaning of their byres:
A Poor Scholar or a Hedge Schoolmaster
Copied from tattered book upon that page
For lads who sat here by the fireside
Generations gone: I took up other pages—
Old yellow broadsheets that were bluntly printed
And sung on streets of hangings and the like:
And there were some that were less public songs.

Another day and I was in a town
Whose buildings were a dingy Market-house,
And Court-house on the grand side. Crowd was there,
But 'Trial' was the muttered word I heard,
'Assize' I heard; there were no beasts
To give men reason for being on the street:
No bargaining. 'He bears a sentence, he.'
I turned round and saw a sunken face,
And eyes that had no hope or light in them—
An old man with a desperate thing to say:
'He bears a sentence.' A young man went
Between the constables, the guards who showed
Some fear of sticks in men's hands or stones
Picked from the street. But there was pain for more
Than one arrest in face that there I looked on. . . .

Back in the days when I was still at school,
Street songs I heard and used the lines I heard
Running beside my hoop as children's rhymes,
Not knowing that the lines came out of conflict
That led to prison cells, demolished houses.
I came to know
The mounting tumult, banners and parades,
And torch-lit meetings, and the high debates
Were all to end a power that could take
Their fields from men who tilled them or who grazed,
The power to turn the cabins built of clay
Back into clay. I looked upon a grapple,
And what was hearsay now was spectacle.
'He bears a sentence!' Often and often
These words were said for many another man.

And then and there a band came into life
With rebel tune that lowered pompousness
Of Court-house and Assize, and made the going
Of one man towards the gaol gate memorable
As though the lines of a great pencil showed it.

And then another turn: red-coated men
On horses and with hounds, their heads held down,
Had come in and were passing by the crowd—
The owners of the countryside were they,
And they were riding with their hounds beside them
To where more mounted men stayed in a field.
Unruffledly they went; then from the field
A bugle rang out and another bugle
With domineering note, and then the hounds
Raised heads in eagerness; I looked towards the field
Where now the mounted men were gathering:
They made a patch of red beyond the town.

The patch of black I saw—Owen Paralon's—
The field he ploughed.—I saw him in the field
Where I went with the lad that brought his meal,
The ploughman's meal such as his father had,
And such as he had in these forty years:
Oat-cakes with butter that was laid as deep
As they were thick, and draughts of buttermilk.
Then watercress. I stepped up to the pool
And gathered leaves that gave the oaten cakes
A tang. When I stood up
The width of country was spread before me,
Coloured with blossom and the green of crop.
I heard the lark's song, and in the distance
Voices that were where household tasks were plied.
A heritage it was, and though some claimed it,
It was for those who could rejoice in it—
And who would come and, standing in this place,
Rejoice, and know that he or she rejoiced?

The ploughman halted, left the plough at stand,
And walked his field as if he still had hold
Of the plough's handles; his head was high—

Ere Beowulf's song
Was from the ships,
Ere Roland had set
The horn to his lips.

In Ogham strokes
A name was writ,
In his that name
Is living yet.

The strokes on the edge
Of the stone might count
The acres he owns
On this bare mount.

But he remembers
The Ogham stone,
And knows that he is
Of the seed of Conn.

The nestling crows had come down on the grass,
And there were squawking, or were lifting up
Their wings. The time had come for me to leave.
Her litter raging, racing, pushing under
Her slack teats, and heading past
To gulp the mash, a sow was at the trough;
A gander stood
Urgent to have his geese get them away
Down to the cleanly pool. I looked into the yard.
All parting's grave because it leaves a doubt
If all has been fulfilled where one has been,
If all can be accomplished where one goes.
Johanna stood to take her leave of me
With a good prayer. Owen Paralon brought out
The big-boned mare, and yoked the outside car.

I mounted, and with Owen Paralon
Across from me, we took the road again
Between the hedgerows, and came to where
The long rails stretched out. 'I know that you will come
Back to us,' Owen Paralon said to me.
'Some time,' 'some time,' 'some time,' the puffing train.

II

Back in the town I turned into the harbour
That I had found; it was a tall dark house
Behind a hedge of variegated laurel,
And I would come to it after my hours
Of fruitless work, and mount the steps and enter
With hopes of great discoveries, and leave it
With thoughts were like a rebels' regiment,
Unled, unbannered, and with pikes for weapons.
I'd walk along an empty quayside then,
Some thought emerging that I'd try to seize.

And that repository of the arcane,
The occult and prophetic, was made before
The century's beginning; some Huguenots,
Strangers in the land, becoming strangers
To their inheritance, had formed it,
But mainly one man who had owned this mansion:
He had known
The one who wrote *Melmoth the Wanderer*,
Fantastic Mathurin, and afterwards
Another of the old community,
Lefanu who wrote *House in the Churchyard*,
And *Uncle Silas* would read the volumes
Of visionaries that were upon the shelves.

And there I'd sit with a few other readers,
Old men who had the pride
That made them strive for erudition
Beyond what others have, some lonely knowledge
Reached by those who leave the commonsense
To others in the street, and so become
Prophets or pedants, forgotten or remembered.

I had been given leave to enter there
Because of service I had done the grandson
Of him who gave the place to coterie,
And there I'd read by light of candles
In tall brass candle-sticks, and under the portrait
Of one in dark robes, banker and ambassador
Whose mind was present to us in these books.

The century that held my twenty years
Came to an end, and as I walked the quayside,
Alone, I felt within
Gropings for words and measure to give form
To what I'd read, the utterance that closed
The century before, in scene illumined
By the cold light that was on frozen seas,
"Farewell to you who die for Kings of earth,
Farewell, ye races without native land.
Farewell, ye lands without a people in them"—
Seraphita's cry in Balzac's story—

And on that theme some lines of verse came to me—
The theme of proud farewell. I walked along
Between the river and the silent houses
And tried to follow out the argument
On number and infinitude that had stirred
An intellectual wonder as I read.

The century as it came would bring to me
Possession of the lore that was foreshown,
Or so I dreamt, walking along the quayside,
While bells ended the century.

I did not read much further in these books,
Or what I read remained outside my grasp,
For in the daily papers there was news
Of Owen Paralon, how for a speech
Made in a market place that had been cowed
By proclamation, and assembly
Of armed men, he had been arrested
And was in gaol; there was a picture
Of his being hauled from seat of outside-car
By constables.
When the time came for me to get my leave
From office work, I left the town behind,
And went to visit him, now out of gaol.

The big-boned mare, the outside-car were there,
But when we started off between the hedge-rows
We did not go as steadily and well,
As at first time. A servant-boy,
And not Owen Paralon, drove the outside car.
He came to me
With friendship in his face, his hands outstretched,
Johanna with him, and all their words were kind.

Seeing the bog-deal blaze upon the hearth,
The silver cup in place upon the shelf,
I thought things had not changed, and then I knew
Something was altered in Owen Paralon.
Though still his stature and his features were
Commanding, there was gauntness in his look:

Not as a man out of the Fenian stories
As I had seen him when he came to me,
With fullness of heroic energy,
Did he appear as he stood on the floor
Of his own house; it seemed as though the years
That had kept distance from him now flowed in,
So that a prime that had been barely reached
A little while before, was past for him.
He was a man whom harrassment had broken
To some degree. We sat to dinner:
Our felon told us of the bed he'd slept on
Too short for his full length, and of the 'skilly'
The prison porridge that was made so thin
There was no mouthful in it.

    Later on,
Seated with company beside the hearth
A neighbour said, "All we went through
To win our land will be like stories told
Of wars and insurrections long ago.
Our children who'll listen to such tales
Will see the Big House as empty as the Castle."
"Something is lost in every change that comes,"
Owen Paralon replied, "and I can tell you
This house had once more life between its walls
Than it or house around will see again."

He spoke again: "A carter mending harness
Was on that bench, and where the light was best,
The threasher using cords to bind the flail,"
And then went on, "A woman carding wool
Was there, a girl spinning yarn,
And there were others that the neighbours honored
Around the hearth, the poet and the scholar,
The pilgrim, too, the story teller.

And in the book the hearthside makes a place
Where he or she whose ways were on the roads,
Coming in, could have a warm place to sleep
On bed of heather-tops. But who is left
To tell what was the look of man or woman
Who made stir here, or what discourse they had"
And there she was, the woman of the house
Attending them, and taking from the ovens
The high brown bread, baked from the wheat we reaped
In bottom field and ground in mill above us,
To serve as supper for the labourers,
And set beside the warm bread, the butter,
A mug of milk and goose egg at each platter."
"A well stocked house," A neighbour said, and one
"I mind the songs, I mind the discourse here.
But who'll have memory of them when we're gone?

And, later, when the neighbours had gone home,
And my two friends had left me for their bed,
I still kept place beside the covered fire.
I was alone,
But there were people with me, men and women
Who had abodes, who had a history,
And work, and humours, and the moiety
Of poetry tradition keeps in trust.
And I could hear,
The door being open, certain birds that flew
Between the clouds and bog, and I could hear
The cattle moving in the byre, the horses
Stirring in their short sleeps, and while I sat,
My mind took to itself a murmuring,
And there were words that it was fitted to,
Words that turned in furrows or in verses,
And took a shape, and went with certainty
Among surprises, and became a poem.

And the next day, when we went on the knoll,
To where the sheep were, I told my poem
To my companion, Owen Paralon
And he made much of it: in deed it was
Raised up, as if a cow or horse of his
Was brought on as the crowning of the fair.

"'Tis long since we'd a poet hereabouts,"
He told me solemnly, and then he said,
"It is a day for me when I can show
As poet, one who comes beneath my roof."
And then I knew
That I was given a place whose vacancy
Was oft disturbing. There was no commission
As for a magistrate, no ordination
As for a priest, but still tradition held
That every place that had a country name
Should own a poet, and on Owen Paralon's
Warrant, I was the poet of this place.

From the one poem I made, another came,
And my investiture became my guidance —
(It was my drinking from the silver cup
Passed round the company in Owen Paralon's)
And later, when my employment changed,
And I was sent about the countryside
To register the changes in the land's
Ownership, I went into the houses,
And on the by ways, and to fairs and markets,
And followed roads unsettled men went on.

I made poems out of glimpses I was given
Of days and nights of women and of men,
And often with the words they spoke to me

Or verses they remembered. I did not neglect
To "prove my poetry," as in bygone times,
So in the springtime I would close a circuit
And go between the hedgerows when the whins
Were golden, and would come to where the crows
Fed their discordant broods, and go within
Owen Paralon's, and to a company
Whose minds the words enlivened as the turf
Down breaking made a kindling in the ash
— told my poems, and as they say in stories,
The ford I found, they found the stepping-stones.

Circuit One · The House

I

A GAUNT-BUILT woman and her son-in-law
A broad-faced fellow, with such flesh as shows
Nothing but easy nature, and his wife,
The woman's daughter, who spills all her talk
Out of a wide mouth and who has eyes as grey
As Connemara, where the mountain-ash
Shows berries red indeed: they enter now
Our country-singers, and your Hedge-school Master
Brings them upon your floor, with due respect
For company and song. . . . My good woman!
And, if you will, some legend handed down.

—I'll sing the song, sir—

Tonight you see my face—
Maybe never more you'll gaze
On the one that for you left his friends and kin;
For by the hard commands
Of the lord that rules these lands
On a ship I'll be borne from Cruckmaelinn!

Oh, you know your beauty bright
Has made him think delight
More than from any fair one he will gain;
Oh, you know that all his will
Strains and strives around you till
As the hawk upon his hand you are as tame!

Then she to him replied:
'I'll no longer you deny,
And I'll let you have the pleasure of my charms,
For tonight I'll be your bride,
And whatever may betide
It's we will lie in one another's arms!'

19

You should not sing
With body doubled up and face aside—
There is a climax here—'It's we will lie—'
Hem—passionate!—And what does your daughter sing?

—A song I like when I do climb bare hills—
'Tis all about a hawk—

No bird that sits on rock or bough
Has such a front as thine;
No King that has made war his trade
Such conquest in his eyne!
I know thee rock-like on the rock
Where none can mark a shape;
I climb, but thou dost climb with wings,
And like a wish escape,
    She said,
And like a wish escape!

No maid that kissed his bonny mouth
Of another mouth was glad;
Such pride was in our Chieftain's eyes,
Such countenance he had!
But since they made him fly our rocks,
Thou, Creature, art my quest—
Then lift me with thy steady eyes,
If then to tear my breast,
    She said,
If then to tear my breast!

The songs they have
Are from the time when lords were lords indeed,
With castles in their keeping; they are songs
Women will keep while men will have them new
As minted money. What song have you, young man?

—A song my father had, sir. It was sent him
From across the sea, and there was a letter with it,
Asking my father to put it to a tune
And sing it all roads. He did that, in troth,
And five pounds of tobacco were sent with the song
To fore-reward him. I'll sing it for you now—
'The Baltimore Exile'.

The house I was bred in—ah, does it remain?
Low walls and loose thatch standing lone in the rain,
With the clay of the walls coming through in its stain,
Like the blackbird's left nest in the briar!

Does a child there give heed to the song of the lark,
As it lifts and it drops till the fall of the dark,
When the heavy-foot kine trudge home from the park,
Or do none but the red-shank now listen?

The sloe-bush, I know, grows close to the well,
And its blossoms long-lasting are there, I can tell,
When the kid that was yeaned when the first ones befell
Can jump to the ditch that they grow on!

But there's silence on all. Then do none ever pass
On the way to the fair, or the pattern, or mass?
Do the grey-coated lads drive the ball through the grass
And speed to the sweep of the hurl?

O youths of my land! Then will no Bolivar
Ever muster your ranks for delivering war?
Will your hopes become fixed and beam like a star?
Will they pass like the mist from your fields?

The swan and the swallow, the cuckoo and crake
May visit my land and find hillside and lake,
And I send my song—I'll not see her awake—
I'm a bird too old to uncage now!

The settle at the hearth—come to it, Singers—
The Master's bidding! You'll find there will be room
Along the table for you ere you leave
And here's a silver bit for each of you—
The Master's gift.

And may we meet his like
Every day's end!

A song is more lasting than the voice of the birds!
A word is more lasting than the riches of the world!

I I

MY grandfather, Downal Baun,
Had the dream that comes three times:
He dreamt it first when, a servant-boy,
He lay by the nets and the lines:

In the house of Fargel More,
And by Fargel's ash-strewn fire,
When Downal had herded the kine in the waste,
And had foddered them down in the byre:

And he dreamt the dream when he lay
Under sails that were spread to the main,
When he took his rest amid dusky seas
On the deck of a ship of Spain:

And the dream came to him beneath
The roof he had raised in his pride,
When beside him there lay and dreamt of her kin,
His strange and far-brought bride.

He had dreamt three times of the treasure
That fills a broken tale—
The hoard of the folk who had raised the mounds,
Who had brewed the heather ale:

And he knew by the thrice-come dream
He could win that hoard by right,
If he drew it out of the lake by a rush
Upon Saint Brighid's night,
By rushes strung to the yoke of an ox
That had never a hair of white !

So Downal, the silent man,
Went to many a far-off fair,
And he bought him an ox no man could say
Was white by a single hair:

And he came to the edge of the lake
When no curlew cried overhead:
Silent and bare from the shaking reeds
The lake-water spread:

And he found it afloat on the current,
The yoke that was hard for the brunt;
And he took the yoke and he bound it
Upon the ox its front:

It was strung with a tie of rushes:
He saw the burthened net:
By the push of the ox, by the pull of the rush
Towards the shore the hoard was set.

Gold cups for Downal Baun,
Sword-hilts that Kings' hands wore !
O, the rush-string drew the treasure
Till the ripples reached the shore !

Red rings for Downal's bride,
White silver for her rein!
But weight was laid on each mesh of the net
And the lake held her own again!

'I will break their strength,' he cried,
'Though they put forth all of their might,
For to me was given the yoke and the dream
And the ox with no hair of white.'

He whispered, 'Labour, O Creature,'
The wide-horned head was set;
The runnels came from eyes, nose and mouth;
The thick hide was all sweat.

'Forgive me the goad, O Creature!'
It hunched from foreleg to flank;
Heaved; they the yoke on the forehead
Split, and the treasure sank,
And Downal was left with the broken yoke,
And the silent ox on the bank.

He turned the ox to the sedges;
He took it and held the yoke up;
Then he flung it far back in the water
Of the dark mountain-cup:

And he shouted, 'Doomsters, I know
Till five score years from this night
The treasure is lost, and I trow
My ox has a hair of white.'

He stood by the ox its front,
And brute and man were still,
And Downal saw lights burn on the lake
And fires within the hill.

He turned: a horse was beside him;
It was white as his ox was black:
Who rode it was a woman:
She paced with him down the track:

And along a road not straitened
By ridge or tower or wood,
And past where the Stones of Morna
Like headless giants stood:

And then on the night of Saint Brighid
The prayer of her vigil he said,
When he looked on the white-horsed woman
And saw the sign on her head.

'The silks that I wear to my elbows,
The golden clasps at my side,
The silver upon my girdle—
I will give them for your bride.'

'Such gear, O horned Woman,
Makes due a pledge, I deem.'
'Nay, I will gift you freely
And you shall tell your dream.'

'They say that whoever tells not
His dream till he hears the birds—
That man will know the prophecies
In long-remembered words.'

'Nay. Tell your dream. Then this hazel
Distaff your wife will gain.'
'The thing that comes in silence,' he said,
'In silence must remain.'

'O dream-taught man,' said the woman—
She stood where the willows grew,
A woman from the country
Where the cocks never crew !

'O dream-taught man,' said the woman—
She stayed by a running stream—
'As wise, as wise as the man,' she said,
'Who never told his dream.'

Then, swift as the flight of the sea-pie,
White woman, white horse, went away,
And Downal passed his haggard
And faced the spear of the day:

And brought his ox to the byre,
And gave it a measure of straw—
'A white hair you have,' said Downal,
'But my plough you are fit to draw;

And for no dream you'll be burthened,
And for none you will bear the yoke.'
Then he lifted the latch of his house-door,
And his bride at his coming awoke
And he drank the milk that she gave him
And the bread she made he broke.

The ox was his help thereafter
When he ploughed the upland and lea
And the growth on the Ridge of the Black Ox
Had a place in men's memory.

And my grandfather, Downal Baun,
Henceforth grew in gains where he stood—
Strong salmon of Lough Oughter,
Grey hawk of the shady wood!

     .   .   .   .   .

Tomorrow we'll gather the rushes
And plait them beside the fire,
And make Saint Brighid's crosses
To hang in the room and the byre.

III

MY eyelids red and heavy are
With bending o'er the smouldering peat.
I know the Aeneid now by heart,
My Virgil read in cold and heat,
In loneliness and hunger smart;
  And I know Homer, too, I ween,
  As Munster poets know Ossian.

And I must walk this road that winds
'Twixt bog and bog, while east there lies
A city with its men and books;
With treasures open to the wise,
Heart-words from equals, comrade-looks;
  Down here they have but tale and song,
  They talk Repeal the whole night long.

'You teach Greek verbs and Latin nouns,'
The dreamer of Young Ireland said,
'You do not hear the muffled call,
The sword being forged, the far-off tread
Of hosts to meet as Gael and Gall*—
  What good to us your wisdom-store,
  Your Latin verse, your Grecian lore?'

And what to me is Gael or Gall?
Less than the Latin or the Greek—
I teach these by the dim rush-light
In smoky cabins night and week.
But what avail my teaching slight?
  Years hence, in rustic speech, a phrase,
  As in wild earth a Grecian vase!

* Gall: *foreigner.*

27

IV

'THE blackbird's in the briar,
The seagull's on the ground—
They are nests, and they're more than nests,' he said,
'They are tokens I have found.

There, where the rain-dashed briar
Marks an empty glade,
The blackbird's nest is seen,' he said,
'Clay-rimmed, uncunningly made.

By shore of the inland lake,
Where surgeless water shoves,
The seagulls have their nests,' he said,
'As low as cattles' hooves.'

I heard a poet say it,
The sojourner of a night;
His head was up to the rafter
Where he stood in candles' light.

'Your houses are like the seagulls'
Nests—they are scattered and low;
Like the backbirds' nests in briars,' he said,
'Uncunningly made—even so:

But close to the ground are reared
The wings that have widest sway,
And the birds that sing best in the wood,' he said,
'Were reared with breasts to the clay.

You've wildness—I've turned it to song;
You've strength—I've turned it to wings;
The welkin's for your conquest then,
The wood to your music rings.'

I heard a poet say it,
The sojourner of a night;
His head was up to the rafter,
Where he stood in candles' light.

V

WE wander now who marched before,
Hawking our bran from door to door,
While other men from the mill take their flour:
 So it is to be an Old Soldier.

Old, bare and sore, we look on the hound
Turning upon the stiff frozen ground,
Nosing the mould, with the night around:
 So it is to be an Old Soldier.

And we who once rang out like a bell,
Have nothing now to show or to sell;
Old bones to carry, old stories to tell:
 So it is to be an Old Soldier.

VI

WHO will bring the red fire
Unto a new hearth?
Who will lay the wide stone
On the waste of the earth?

Who is fain to begin
To build day by day—
To raise up his house
Of the moist yellow clay?

There is clay for the making
Moist in the pit,
There are horses to trample
The rushes through it.

And a tree on the ridge grows
To be his roof-tree
The branches across it
House-rafters will be.

And saplings that bend
Will be woven between;
O'er them thatch of the crop
Shall be heavy and clean.

(He shall stand on his roof
Against the wind's swell,
As he plies through the straw
The scallops of hazel!)

I speak unto him
Who in dead of the night
Sees the red streaks
In the ash deep and white;

While around him he hears
Men stir in their rest,
And the stir of the child
That is close to the breast!

He shall arise;
He shall go forth alone,
Lay stone on the earth
And bring fire to stone.

VII

I'M glad to lie on a sack of leaves
By a wasted fire and take my ease.
For the wind would strip me bare as a tree—
The wind would blow oul' age upon me,
And I'm dazed with the wind, the rain, and the cold!
If I had only the good red gold
To buy me the comfort of a roof,
And under the thatch the brown of the smoke!
I'd lie up in my painted room
Until my hired girl would come;
And when the sun had warmed my walls
I'd rise up in my silks and shawls,
And break my fast beside the fire.
And I'd watch them that had to sweat
And shiver for shelter and what they ate—
The farmer digging in the fields,
The beggars going from gate to gate,
The horses striving with their loads,
And all the sights upon the roads.

I'd live my lone without clan nor care,
And none around me to crave a share;
The young have mocking, impudent ways,
And I'd never let them a-nigh my place,
And a child has often a pitiful face.
I'd give the rambling fiddler rest,
And for me he would play his best,
And he'd have something to tell of me
From the Moat of Granard down to the sea!
And, though I'd keep distant, I'd let in
Oul' women who would card and spin,
And clash with me, and I'd hear it said,
'Mor, who used to carry her head
As if she was a lady bred,

Has little enough in her house, they say;
And such a one's child I saw on the way
Scaring crows from a crop, and glad to get
In a warmer house, the bit to eat—
Oh, none are safe and none secure,
And it's well for some whose bit is sure!'

I'd never grudge them the weight of their lands
If I had only the good red gold
To huggle between my breast and my hands!

VIII

THE moon-cradle's rocking and rocking
Where a cloud and a cloud go by,
Silently rocking and rocking
The moon-cradle out in the sky.

Then comes the lad with the hazel
And the folding star's in the rack,
'Night's a good herd' to the cattle,
He sings, 'She brings all things back.'

But the bond-woman there by the boorie*
Sings with a heart grown wild
How a hundred rivers are flowing
Between herself and her child.

'The geese, even they, trudge homeward
That have their wings and the waste,
Let your thoughts be on Night the Herder,
And be quiet for a space.'

* Boorie: *shelter for cattle.*

THE HOUSE

The moon-cradle's rocking and rocking,
Where a cloud and a cloud go by,
Silently rocking and rocking
The moon-cradle out in the sky,

The snipe they are crying and crying
Liadine, liadine, liadine.
Where no track's on the bog they are flying—
A lonely dream will be mine!

Circuit Two · Field and Road

I

SUNSET and silence! A man; around him earth savage, earth
     broken;
Beside him two horses, a plough!

Earth savage, earth broken, the brutes, the dawn-man there in the
     sunset,
And the plough that is twin to the sword, that is founder of cities!

'Brute-tamer, plough-maker, earth-breaker! Canst hear?
    There are ages between us—
Is it praying you are as you stand there alone in the sunset?

Surely our sky-born gods can be naught to you, earth-child and
     earth-master—
Surely your thoughts are of Pan, or of Wotan, or Dana?

Yet why give thought to the gods? Has Pan led your brutes where
     they stumble?
Has Dana numbed pain of the child-bed, or Wotan put hands to
     your plough?

What matter your foolish reply? O man standing lone and bowed
     earthward,
Your task is a day near its close. Give thanks to the night-giving
     god.'

Slowly the darkness falls, the broken lands blend with the
     savage;
The brute-tamer stands by the brutes, a head's breadth only above
     them.

A head's breadth? Aye, but therein is hell's depth and the height
     up to heaven,
And the thrones of the gods and their halls, their chariots, purples,
     and splendours.

II

STRIDE the hill, Sower,
Up to the sky-ridge,
Casting the seed
While silence holds houses !

Below in the darkness,
The slumbers of mothers,
The cradles at rest,
The fire-seed sleeping
Deep in white ashes.

And you casting the seed
As on mornings unmemoried,
Up to the sky-ridge,
MacCeacht or MacGrian ! *

* *Son of the Plough, Son of the Sun: traditional agrarian personages.*

III

A CROOKED man stands in the gap beside a holly tree,
And like a whetstone on a blade, his scraping words to me,
'The handles grip, you gawky lad, till swathe to swathe you lay,
For scythe must sweep from hedge to hedge to win the spalpeen's
    pay.
      From hedge to hedge, and quick at that,
      To win the spalpeen's * pay.'

* Spalpeen: *a hired scythesman.*

The rushes at the river bend have talk of something else:
'Before you turn your scythe at all, look on the springing grass!
What do you know who've only seen the stone-bound fields of
    Clare,
How grass makes green the acres of the uplands of Kildare?
            For here's the leafy hedges,
            And the uplands of Kildare!'

The ash tree in her garden was growing fresh and green,
And by the ash tree there she stood, commanding as a queen.
'Take up your scythe or reaping-hook.' I turned from her away,
To travel up and travel down and win the spalpeen's pay,
            They'll turn to him, they'll turn to him,
            Who brings the spalpeen's pay.

A stalwart man walks on the field, his arms have steady swing,
With flash of blade the grass is laid as even as a string.
Before him is the meadow's crown as garden's face more bright,
The growing grass, the summer grass, the grass wrapped in sun-
    light!
            The growth of grass, the sunlit grass,
            The grass that claims his scythe.

Corncrake, 'twas often I heard you in the first red streak of the
    day,
Me, with my melodies wasting, and you at the height of your play,
And now I will narrow your meadow to win me the spalpeen's
    pay.
No craking from you will forbid me to mow for the spalpeen's
    pay.
            You've craked long enough in our grasses
            And my word to you now is 'away'!

IV

ONE man was still upon the ridge,
Spading potatoes from their clay;
The hareskin cap upon his head
Made him look wild—a man astray.

Creel-loads and pot-fulls he struck out—
Potatoes in the furrow thronged,
But still, as though the fading light,
The spended light, a spadesman wronged

He dug—the spade went down, and then,
Went down again; went down, went down;
The only sound came to us there,
His spade in clay, his spade on stone.

One said, 'These tenants were so racked,
With rent on field, on bog, on shore,
There was no season but they saw
The bailiff's shadow on the door.

When others mustered to proclaim
With band and banner their leagued oath
To break the tenants' bondage, theirs—
How could this parish show its troth?

So poor they were—and this will show,
They had no share in parish band,
Neither a banner could they buy,
To give them name or prove their stand.

Then one bethought that blazing turfs
Set on pitchforks would do as well
As lettered banner with device,
Or fife-and-drum's uplifting swell.

And so they did, and I have heard
The ballad-singers praise the lads,
The pitchfork men who lifted up
The standard of the blazing sods.'

I saw behind our man a line
Of parish folk, their pitchforks down,
Grasping the foregone spades to dig
A harvest that was all their own.

And there the man in hareskin cap
Toiling as though to lay with spade
The ghost of want, the ghost of blight
In the long furrow they had made.

But let that be! I single out
From folk of parish, odd and even
The man upon the ridge alone,
The man with spade, the man hard-driven.

V

To Meath of the pastures,
From wet hills by the sea,
Through Leitrim and Longford,
Go my cattle and me.

I hear in the darkness
Their slipping and breathing—
I name them the by-ways
They're to pass without heeding;

Then the wet, winding roads,
Brown bogs with black water,
And my thoughts on white ships
And the King o' Spain's daughter.

O farmer, strong farmer!
You can spend at the fair,
But your face you must turn
To your crops and your care;

And soldiers, red soldiers!
You've seen many lands,
But you walk two by two
And by captain's commands!

O the smell of the beasts,
The wet wind in the morn,
And the proud and hard earth
Never broken for corn!

And the crowds at the fair,
The herds loosened and blind,
Loud words and dark faces,
And the wild blood behind!

(O strong men with you best
I would strive breast to breast,
I could quiet your herds
With my words, with my words!)

I will bring you, my kine,
Where there's grass to the knee,
But you'll think of scant croppings
Harsh with salt of the sea.

VI

'LOST,' 'lost,' the beeves, the bullocks,
The cattle men sell and buy,
Crowded upon the Fair Green,
Low to the lightless sky.

'Live,' 'live,' and 'here,' 'here,' the blackbird
From the top of the bare ash tree,
Over the acres whistles
With beak of yellow blee.

And climbing, turning and climbing
His little stair of sound,
'Content,' 'content,' from the low hedge
The redbreast sings in a round.

And I with pack to carry,
Will fare with all the rest,
With thoughts of luck and labour
And bargain in my breast,

As when I come to cheapen
Her moiety of wool,
That earns for the farmer's wife
Her looked-for Paisley shawl.

The bare hedge bright with rain-drops
That have not fallen down,
The golden-crowded whin-bush—
Nor know these things my own!

VII

AND when she comes she'll stand beside the herd
Holding a halter while I lay the brand
On colt and filly; she'll not speak a word,
But with her face like a dark wood she'll stand.
Her eyes upon the cairn where they'll graze
Her colts and fillies on the hilly waste,
She will not turn to me with look or word.

Why do I look for fire to brand these foals,
What do I need when all around is fire?
And now she comes, carrying the lighted coals
And branding-tool—she who is my desire.
What need have I for what is in her hands?
If I lay hand upon a hide, it brands,
And grass and trees and hedges all are fire!

VIII

IN companies or lone
They bend their heads, their hands
They busy with their gear,
Accomplishing the stitch
That turns the stocking heel
Or closes up the toe,
  These knitters at their doors.
Their talk's of nothing else
But what was told before
Sundown and gone sundown,
While goats bleat from the hill,
And men are tramping home
  By knitters at their doors.

And we who go this way
A benediction take
From hands that ply this task
For the ten-thousandth time—
    Of knitters at their doors.
Since we who deem our days
Most varied, come to own
That all the works we do
Repeat a wonted toil:
May it be done as theirs
Who turn the stocking-heel
And close the stocking-toe
With grace and in content,
    These knitters at their doors.

IX

WATER, I did not seek you,
Water of hollow stone;
I crossed no man's acre to find you—
You were where my geese lie down.

I bring you across the threshold—
My house is quiet, apart;
I have not called for a woman
To take her place at my hearth.

The numbness that leaves me vacant
Of thought and will and deed
Like the moveless clock that I gaze on—
It will go where the ravens breed.

I dip my finger and sprinkle,
And three times over I say,
'Chance-bound and chance-found water
Will take a numbness away.'

In search there is no warrant,
By chance is the charm shown:
Water, I did not seek you,
Water of hollow stone!

Gallant amongst the gallant,
I shall speak and lead and strive.
Empty the stone! On the morrow
I shall rise with spirit alive.

X

OH I wish the sun was bright in the sky,
And the fox was back in his den O!
For always I'm hearing the passing by
Of the terrible robber men O!
   Of the terrible robber men.

Oh what does the fox carry over the rye,
When it's bright in the morn again O!
And what is it making the lonesome cry
With the terrible robber men O!
   With the terrible robber men.

Oh I wish the sun was bright in the sky,
And the fox was back in his den O!
For always I'm hearing the passing by
Of the terrible robber men O!
   Of the terrible robber men.

Circuit Three · Things More Ancient

Fore-piece

LEAVING where I was quartered—
A gaunt, grey town that has a history—
(And I was quartered there because a vein
Of silver owned by one in Vera Cruz
Who'd sailed from this grey town was in dispute,
And I could gather there the recollections
Of those who'd known him in a long-lost youth:
Distant relations whose distant visitations
Seemed bound in vellum for their parlour tables).
Leaving the gaunt houses,
I came upon a road where there were hedges,
Thorn, hazel, oak, whin, ash and elm
Blackthorn, boar-tree, and the wild rose
That kept the tang of forest they supplanted,
A road that had a thousand-year old name.

I saw a woman and three men before me:
They walked as pilgrims walk—as on an errand
That is not, as the story-tellers prelude,
In your time or in my time, but in some time
That stands outside the thousands of our days.
This was a day
When they would measure thousand petty acts
Against an act made in the face of God.

The four were round the well,
And on their knees when I came to the place
Of pilgrimage. I went to what was left
Of the saint's cell, and stayed within it.
The little wren
That often earned praise from such old saint
Sang in the solitude that Time had spread.

And as the nightingale sang in Pehlevi,
The wren sang in the Irish of old books,
'A flowing sea of miracles and signs,
The nursing-knee of wisdom,' and again,
'A hundred mysteries his heart is shrine of.
His place will be until the Day of Judgement
Honoured.' I heard the invocations
Of those around the well, and looked upon
Hedra Hibernica that is kind to ruins
And wished to make petitions as they made them.

The great cross—
I marvelled how it stood almost entire:
Its front and back,
Its sides and circle were inscribed with figures
But little raised above the stone itself,
Or worn down to it—massive, circled,
Enscrolled and storied, something greatly wrought
Out of that Ireland whose fortune was soon lost.

The pilgrims
Now moved amongst the graves that were their fathers',
For they were remnants of the old stock
That lived in Glens beyond; they had the right
To ancient places for their burials.
They spoke to me; they had
The mother-tongue. Something outlasting
The toils and losses that are the portion
Of those who live on acres fenced with stones
Was in the woman's face, giving civility
To looks and bearing. 'And you will come
To see us in our Glen,' she said to me,
'And we will tell you of the saints were here.'
And a man said, 'We'll sing you the old songs
When you come to us.' I promised that I would.

I did. And after that I spent a day
Going up and down the fair that that gaunt town
Takes in as country cousin (Glens and Fair
Are set out in the Poet's Circuits here)
And after I had traced
The heirs of him who found the vein of silver
In Vera Cruz, I went back to the place
Of pilgrimage, and stood before the great
Antiquity that was the figured Cross.

Saint Brighid's Day it was, the first of Spring.
The light that makes the fields, the thatch of houses
Enlivened, was upon the stone—
The palpitating light of Ireland.
I knew the Craftsman saw them in this light,
Each figure with a life that was its own:
A figure in a boat, and he was Brendan
Who sailed into the Western Sea before
A name was given to that width of water.
And there were other figures that had names.
Then on Saint Brighid's Day when the sun takes
A 'cock's step', and 'tis Spring, I went within
The Saint's own cell, and, conscious of the light,
I stayed there, and reworded an old poem—
A poem that had this light
Moving across the countryside, a poem
Made in the century the Cross was made.

I

MAY day! Surpassing time!
The lovely colours stay,
And where there's shaft of light
The blackbird rounds his lay.

The cuckoo flies and calls,
That bird of dusty hue,
From branch and then from hedge,
'All, May-time, welcome you!'

Lesser the river goes,
The heather tresses spread,
And horses seek the pool:
The bog-down lifts its head.

The sail is far away:
But near—a strenuous bard,
The corncrake in long grass,
Makes much of his one word.

Peace, peace is over all,
And where the swallows skim,
One hears the rushes talk;
The quagmire sucks its rim.

The sea lies smooth these times,
The ocean-tides are lulled;
The deer makes sudden start;
The blossoms fill the wold.

Now like the raven's coat,
The bog is seen around,
The trout leaps in the stream;
Strong is the hero's bound.

And in the clear-skyed month
Man comes into his own;
The maiden in fair pride
Buds, and her beauty's known.

The haze is on the lake,
And there's a harp of might—
The forest in the breeze:
The colours take the height.

And in the pool below
A virgin with her chant,
The lofty waterfall,
Welcomes the visitant.

On us a longing comes
Horses to mount and ride,
And on the horses, too,
To take their mettled stride.

Bees load themselves from bloom;
The kine go up the hill,
Dry mud upon their flanks;
The ants bear all they will.

The water-flag is gold
Where shaft of light strikes down,
And up, above us all,
A singing fellow's gone—

The lark. And all are told
This is the season's prime;
Welcome, the songster shrills,
May day, surpassing time!

II

THREE heroes, we, at the hunting,
The chase on the slope of Slieve Gua,
Started a stag from the oak wood
That was pearly with fresh morning dew—

His like for height and for antlers
On the heath of Gua never was
In all the days of our hunting—
A lithe stag eating young grass!

We loosed them, the dogs for that stag:
What swiftness they had on that day!
But no gain on that chief did we make
Till he reached Slieve Mish, its green brae—

'Twas there he fell to our spears
Fian, I, and Oscar—
In all the Fian there were not
Three heroes as good as we were!

The hours have stolen flesh and bone,
And left a changeling here:
And where is he who had the pride
To chase the bounding deer?

Four feeble bones are left to me,
And the basket of my breast,
And I am mean and ugly now
As the scald flung from the nest.

The briars drag me at the knees,
The brambles go within,
And often do I feel him turn,
The old man in my skin.

The strength is carded from my bones,
The swiftness drained from me,
And all the living thoughts I had
Are like far ships at sea!

III

NOT fingers that ere felt
Fine things within their hold
Drew needles in and through,
And smoothed out the fold,
And put the hodden patch
Upon the patch of grey—
Unseemly is the garb
That's for my back today.

Light of hand and apt,
And companionable—
Seven score women, Mór,
I had at my call,
Who am today begrudged
The blink of candle-light
To put it on, the garb
That leaves me misbedight.

A blue Norse hood I owned
The time I watched the turns
And feats of Clann O'Neill—
We drank from goblet-horns;
A crimson cloak I wore
When, with Niall the King,
I watched the horses race
At Limerick in the Spring.

In Tara of King Niall
The gold was round the wine,
And I was given the cup—
A furze-bright dress was mine;
And now this clout to wear
When I rise to sup whey,
With root-like stitches through
The hodden on the grey!

No more upon the board
Candles for kings are lit,
No more can I bid her,
And her bring gowning fit;
The bramble is no friend—
It pulls at me and drags;
This thorny ground is mine
Where briars tear my rags!

IV

TOMORROW I will bend the bow:
My soul shall have her mark again,
My bosom feel the archer's strain.
No longer pacing to and fro
With idle hands and listless brain:
As goes the arrow, forth I go.
My soul shall have her mark again,
My bosom feel the archer's strain:
Tomorrow I will bend the bow.
   —Spoke Ishmael son of Hagar so
    When he had mourned her on the plain,
    And all was left him was his bow.

V

I KNOW you, Crane:
I, too, have waited,
Waited until my heart
Melted to little pools around my feet!

Comer in the morning ere the crows,
Shunner,
Searcher—
Something find for me!
The pennies that were laid upon the eyes
Of old, wise men I knew.

V I

A GOOD stay-at-home season is Autumn: then there's work to be
joined in by all:
Though the fawns, where the brackens make covert, may range
away undeterred,
The stags that were lone upon hillocks now give heed to the call,
To the bellowing call of the hinds, and they draw back to the
herd.

A good stay-at-home season is Autumn; the brown world's
marked into fields;
The corn is up to its growth; the acorns teem in the wood;
By the side of the down-fallen fort even the thorn-bush yields
A crop, and there by the rath the hazel nuts drop from a load.

VII

ON the third day from this (Saint Brendan said)
I will be where no wind that filled a sail
Has ever been, and it blew high or low:
For from this home-creek, from this body's close
I shall put forth; make ready, you, to go
With what remains to Cluan Hy-many,
For there my resurrection I'd have be.

But you will know how hard they'll strive to hold
This body o' me, and hold it for the place
Where I was bred, they say, and born and reared.
For they would have my resurrection here,
So that my sanctity might be matter shared
By every mother's son the tribeland polled
Who lived and died and mixed into the mould.

So you will have to use all canniness
To bring this body to its burial
When in your hands I leave what goes in clay:
The wagon that our goods are carried in—
Have it yoked up between the night and day,
And when the breath is from my body gone,
Bear body out, the wagon lay it on;

And cover it with gear that's taken hence—
'The goods of Brendan is what's here,' you'll say
To those who'll halt you; they will pass you then:
Tinkers and tailors, soldiers, farmers, smiths,
You'll leave beside their doors—all those thwart men
For whom my virtue was a legacy
That they would profit in, each a degree—

As though it were indeed some chalice, staff,
Crozier or casket, that they might come to,

And show to those who chanced upon the way,
And have, not knowing how the work was done
In scrolls and figures and in bright inlay:
Whence came the gold and silver that they prize,
The blue enamels and the turquoises!

I, Brendan, had a name came from the sea—
I was the first who sailed the outer main,
And past all forelands and all fastnesses!
I passed the voiceless anchorets, their isles,
Saw the ice-palaces upon the seas,
Mentioned Christ's name to men cut off from men,
Heard the whales snort, and saw the Kraken!

And on a wide-branched, green, and glistening tree
Beheld the birds that had been angels erst:
Between the earth and heaven 'twas theirs to wing:
Fallen from High they were, but they had still
Music of Heaven's Court: I heard them sing:
Even now the island of the unbeached coast
I see, and hear the white, resplendent host!

For this they'd have my burial in this place,
Their hillside, and my resurrection be
Out of the mould that they with me would share.
But I have chosen Cluan for my ground—
A happy place! Some grace came to me there:
And you, as you go towards it, to men say,
Should any ask you on that long highway:

'Brendan is here, who had great saints for friends:
Ita, who reared him on a mother's knee,
Enda, who from his fastness blessed his sail:
Then Brighid, she who had the flaming heart,
And Colum-cille, prime of all the Gael:
Gildas of Britain, wisest child of light.'
And saying this, drive through the falling night.

VIII

FIRST, make a letter like a monument—
An upright like the fast-held hewn stone
Immovable, and half-rimming it
The strength of Behemoth his neck-bone,
And underneath that yoke, a staff, a rood
Of no less hardness than the cedar wood.

Then, on a page made golden as the crown
Of sainted man, a scripture you enscroll
Blackly, firmly, with the quickened skill
Lessoned by famous masters in our school,
And with an ink whose lustre will keep fresh
For fifty generations of our flesh.

And limn below it the Evangelist
In raddled coat, on bench abidingly,
Simple and bland: Matthew his name or Mark,
Or Luke or John; the book is by his knee,
And thereby its similitudes: Lion,
Or Calf, or Eagle, or Exalted Man.

The winds that blow around the world—the four
Winds in their colours on your pages join—
The Northern Wind—its blackness interpose;
The Southern Wind—its blueness gather in;
In redness and in greenness manifest
The splendours of the Winds of East and West.

And with these colours on a ground of gold
Compose a circuit will be seen by men
As endless patience, but is nether web
Of endless effort—a strict pattern:
Illumination lighting interlace
Of cirque and scroll, of panel and lattice.

A single line describes them and enfolds,
One line, one course where term there is none,
Which in its termlessness is envoying
The going forth and the return one.
With man and beast and bird and fish therein
Transformed to species that have never been.

With mouth a-gape or beak a-gape each stands
Initial to a verse of miracle,
Of mystery and of marvel (Depth of God!)
That Alpha or Omega may not spell,
Then, finished with these wonders and these signs,
Turn to the figure of your first outlines.

Axal, our angel, has sustained you so
In hand, in brain; now to him seal that thing
With figures many as the days of man,
And colours, like the fire's enamelling—
That baulk, that letter you have greatly reared
To stay the violence of the entering Word!

Adjutorium nostrum, in nomine Domini
Qui fecit caelum et terram.

IX

HERE Pilate's Court is:
None may clatter nor call
Where the Wolf giving suck
To the Twins glares on all.
'Strip Him and scourge Him
Till the flesh shows the blood,
And afterwards nail Him
On cross of wood.'

O Lord
Silence in us the condemning word!

Heaven witnesseth, but only in the heart
Is any aid:
'They know not what they do', and then on Him
The Cross is laid—
The Cross that's wide and long enough to bear
His flesh and bone:
A spectacle upon the crowded way,
The Man goes on.

        The Father's will
May we know also, and may we fulfil!

Beneath the load
The knees quail;
The heart pants
The joints fail;
Almost the bones break;
He faints, His breath being loss;
He sinks beneath the Cross!

        May we
Be mindful of this road to Calvary!

Jesus His Mother meets:
She looks on Him and sees
The Saviour in Her Son:
The Angel's word comes back:
Within her heart she says
'Unto me let this be done!'
Still is she full of grace.

        By us, too, be it won
The grace that brings revelation!

'If He should die upon the road
It were a turn of ill:
'Tis fixed the Crucifixion be
Upon that skull-shaped hill.

Ho, man who looks with pity on
The Man we take to death
Bear you the Cross—I order it—
Until He wins back breath.'

We take
Our hearts being moved, the Cross up for Thy sake!

Down to her face His face He bends:
The helper she, the heartener:
His image in her cloth He leaves;
He leaves it, too, to all like her
Who serve within a little room,
But run to help outside the door,
Who mend and brighten needed things:
He leaves it to good hearts, the Poor!

May we, too, wait
Like her, and help, and be compassionate!

The Spirit is willing—aye,
But weak the flesh put on;
Deadly the Cross's weight;
He stumbles on a stone,
And lies upon the road,
Seeing His Body's blood.

May we
Forget not in these times that agony!

Heavy the Cross is:
He drags beneath its beam,
Yet, Women of Jerusalem,
Weep not for Him:

Weep for your children, rather,
For they that cannot see
The Anointed, the Rejected,
The Saviour, shown ye.

O Lord
Say to us also the arresting word!

The skull-shaped hill is near:
The living light is gone;
The world takes on a change:
He stumbles and falls down,
Knowing the journey's end
Without one to befriend.

O Lord
Bring us to Life according to Thy word!

'Would'st have me share this cloth,
Dividing it with sword?——
Nay, fellow, keep it whole
Until we're left for Guard.
Behind the Cross the dice
We'll throw; who wins will get
What's high enough in price
To pay a tavern debt.'

The vesture that makes one with Thee our soul,
May we keep whole!

'This thong, I know, will last;
Draw out the arm and make it fast;
Through hand and board with strength
Drive nail of mickle length.
Now, King of the Jews, in the sun
Gape, for our work is done.'

God send
That our labours have no evil end !

The birds are flying home,
Now darkened is the sky,
And He hath given up
With that great bitter cry
The ghost, and on the Cross
(His Mother stays by it),
The title rightly His,
King—is writ.

May we draw near
Considering in our hearts what Man is here !

Though pitiful it is to see
The wounds, the broken Body,
(The Body of Him that was
As fair as lily of the grass !)
Though His brow with thorns is riven,
And a spear through the side is driven,
It was for our healing done,
Mother, by the Son !

May we
This Body in its glory come to see !

Now in the tomb is laid
Who had neither house nor hall,
Who in the wide world walked,
And talked with one and all;
Who told the sparrow's worth,
The lily's praises said,
Who kept wakeful in the garden
Now in the tomb is laid.

His Spirit still doth move
On a new way of love !

Prince, by thine own darkened hour,
Live within me, heart and brain;
Let my hands not slip the rein !

Ah, how long ago the hour
Since a comrade rode with me:
Now, a moment, let me see

Thyself, lonely in the dark,
Perfect, without wound nor mark !

X

BLACK tassels, black tassels, upon the green tree,
The high tree, the ash-tree that tops the round hill,
Black tassels, black tassels, and they are the crows.

Red streamers, red streamers along the hedgeways
Where roadways are claubered and stubbles are brown—
Red streamers, red streamers, and they are the haws.

A lone song, a high song that comes from the hedge,
That tries for a round and that falls on the turn—
A short song, the redbreast's, and Samhain's at hand.

Circuit Four · The Glens

I. NOW, COMING ON SPRING *(from the Irish)*

II. RAFTERY

III. SISTER'S LULLABY

IV. GIRLS SPINNING

V. A CONNACHTMAN

VI. A MAN BEREAVED *(from the Scots Gaelic)*

VII. THE POOR GIRL'S MEDITATION *(from the Irish)*

VIII. CROWS

IX. AFTER-PIECE

'There is an hour'

I

Now, coming on Spring, the days will be growing,
And after Saint Bride's Day my sail I will throw;
Since the thought has come to me I fain would be going,
Till I stand in the middle of the County Mayo!

The first of my days will be spent in Claremorris,
And in Balla, beside it, I'll have drinking and sport;
To Kiltimagh, then, I will go on a visit,
And there, I can tell you, a month will be short.

I solemnly swear that the heart in me rises,
As the wind rises up and the mists break below,
When I think upon Carra, and on Gallen down from it,
The Bush of the Mile, and the Plains of Mayo!

Killeadean's my village, and every good's in it;
The rasp and blackberry to set to one's tooth;
And if Raftery stood in the midst of his people,
Old age would go from him, and he'd step to his youth!

II

'Raftery I am,' he said,
'The poet.' Quietly
As one who has no claim to make.
He answered 'Who is he?'

For how might one who stood his ground
In his own self for long
But answer in all simpleness
The usage of a tongue?

69

And when he turned his sightless gaze
On that unknowing lad
He did not have a word to say
Of all the fame he had.

For what is fame beside a loss
That every day can bruise?
The shine upon the buckles broad
Of a worn pair of shoes.

Or even like dance music heard
Upon a rain-swept road
When every lively step has failed
And gone the wishful crowd.

And he who had the mounting words
Now shaped an utterance
In words as simple and as clear
As rain-drops off the thatch.

Betokening that what were left—
The whey-cup and the crust,
The fame, the loss, the pence begrudged—
Were changed to gentle trust.

'Raftery.' A man his name
Had said, and set thereon
The signet of the spirit
Before a jig began.

III

You would not slumber
If laid at my breast:
   You would not slumber.

The river flood beats
The swan from her nest.
   You would not slumber.

Little sister,
I'll rock you to rest.

Times without number
Has cooed the woodquest:
   Times without number.

As oft as she cooed
To me you were pressed:
   Times without number.

Now you'd not slumber
If laid at my breast
   Times without number.

O starling reed-resting,
I'll rock you to rest:
   So you will slumber.

IV

First girl:

Mallo lero iss im bo nero!
Where they're breaking the horses, go find me my lover,
Mallo lero iss im bo baun!

Second girl:

Mallo lero iss im bo nero!
Him with the strong hand I'll bring you over.
Mallo lero iss im bo baun!

First girl:

I'll wait till I hear what he's singing over!

A man's voice sings:

Are they not the good men of Eirinn,
Who give not their thought nor their voice
To fortune, but take without dowry
The maids of their choice?

For the trout has sport in the river
Whether prices be up or low-down
And the salmon, he slips through the water
Not heeding the town!

Then if she, the love of my bosom
Did laugh as she stood by my door,
O I'd rise then and draw her in to me,
With kisses *go leor*!

It's not likely the wind in the tree tops
Would trouble our love nor our rest,
Not the hurrying footsteps would draw her,
My love from my breast!

First girl:

Mallo lero iss im bo nero!
He sings to the girsha* in the hazel-wood cover.
Mallo lero iss im bo baun!

Mallo lero iss im bo nero!
Go where they're shearing and find me my lover.
Mallo lero iss im bo baun!

Second girl:

Mallo lero iss im bo nero!
The newly-come youth is looking straight over!
Mallo lero iss im bo baun!

First girl:

Mallo lero iss im bo nero!
If you mind what he sings, your calf to my clover.
Mallo lero iss im bo baun!

A young man's voice sings:

Once I went over the ocean,
On a ship that was bound for proud Spain:
Some people were singing and dancing,
But I had a heart full of pain.

I'll put now a sail on the lake
That's between my treasure and me,
And I'll sail over the lake
Till I come to the Joyce country.

She'll hear my boat on the shingles,
And she'll hear my step on the land,
And the corncrake deep in the meadow
Will tell her that I'm at hand!

* Girsha: *a young girl.*

The summer comes to Glen Nefin
With heavy dew on the leas,
With the gathering of wild honey
To the tops of all the trees.

In honey and dew the summer
Upon the ground is shed,
And the cuckoo cries until dark
Where my storeen* has her bed!

And if O'Hanlon's daughter
Will give me a welcome kind,
O never will my sail be turned
To a harsh and a heavy wind!

First girl:

Mallo lero iss im bo nero!
Welcome I'll give him over and over.
Mallo lero iss im bo baun!

A young girl sings:

I'd bring you these for dowry—
A field from heather free,
White sheep upon the mountain,
And calves that follow me.

I saw you by the well-side
Upon Saint Finnian's Day;
I thought you'd come and ask for me,
But you kept far away.

Oh, if you ask not for me,
But leave me here instead,
The petticoat in dye-pot here
Will never fast its red

* Storeen: *my little treasure.*

74

For me upon the well-slope
To wear on Finnian's Day—
My dress will be the sheet bleached there,
My place, below the clay!

(There is no answering song)

First girl:

Mallo lero iss im bo nero!
That's all we'll hear till our spinning's over!
Mallo lero iss im bo baun!

V

IT'S my fear that my wake won't be quiet,
Nor my wake-house a silent place:
For who would keep back the hundreds
Who would touch my breast and my face?

For the good men were always my friends,
From Galway back into Clare;
In strength, in sport, and in spending,
I was foremost at the fair;

In music, in song, and in friendship,
In contests by night and by day,
By all who knew it was given to me
That I bore the branch away.

Now let Manus Joyce, my friend
(If he be at all in the place),
Make smooth the boards of the coffin
They will put above my face.

The old men will have their stories
Of all the deeds in my days,
And the young men will stand by the coffin,
And be sure and clear in my praise.

But the girls will stay near the door,
And they'll have but little to say:
They'll bend their heads, the young girls,
And for a while they will pray.

And, going home in the dawning,
They'll be quiet with the boys;
The girls will walk together,
And seldom they'll lift the voice;

And then, between daybreak and dark,
And between the hill and the sea,
Three women, come down from the mountain,
Will raise the keen over me.

But 'tis my grief that I will not hear
When the cuckoo cries in Glenart,
That the wind that lifts when the sails are loosed
Will never lift my heart.

VI

MY wife and my comrade
Will not come at all
Though the pine-tree shall flourish,
The green rush grow tall,
And its cone to the ground
The larch-tree let fall.

She'll not cross my threshold,
Nor with me abide,
Sit down on this doorstep,
Nor lie by my side;
And I'll not hear her sounding
Songs over the din,
Where the people are crowded,
The harvest being in;
Nor see her come lilting
From the field or the fold,
Nor plaiting her long locks
In the young moon nor old.

No more to the hill-tops
Have I heart to go,
Nor to walk through the woods
When the summer sun's low:
Though I weary with delving,
With driving the plough,
I lie on a bed
Sleep has gone from now.

Though goats to their time come
With nobody there;
Though the watched heifer calve
With none to take care,
From the churchyard my woman
Home never will fare.

My house is encumbered,
Unswept my hearth-stone,
The cows low for their milking
In the full height of noon;
No garb is made newly,
No wool is yet spun;
On the floor and untended
Stands the youngling, my son.

On the hills they cry ba-ba,
And bring back their dam;
On the floor and unanswered
Stands the youngling, my lamb,
While I'm saying over
That she'll not come at all
Though the pine-tree shall flourish,
The green rush grow tall,
And its cone to the ground
The larch-tree let fall!

VII

I AM sitting here
Since the moon rose in the night,
Kindling a fire,
And striving to keep it alight.
The folk of the house are lying
In slumber deep;
The geese will be gabbling soon:
The whole of the land is asleep.

May I never leave this world
Until my ill-luck is gone;
Till I have cows and sheep,
And the lad that I love for my own;
I would not think it long,
The night I would lie at his breast,
And the daughters of spite, after that,
Might say the thing they liked best.

Love takes the place of hate,
If a girl have beauty at all:
On a bed that was narrow and high,
A three-month I lay by the wall:
When I bethought on the lad
That I left on the brow of the hill,
I wept from dark until dark,
And my cheeks have the tear-tracks still.

And, O young lad that I love,
I am no mark for your scorn;
All you can say of me is
Undowered I was born:
And if I've no fortune in hand,
Nor cattle and sheep of my own,
This I can say, O lad,
I am fitted to lie my lone!

VIII

THEN, suddenly, I was aware indeed
Of what he said, and was revolving it:
How, in the night, crows often take to wing,
Rising from off the tree-tops in Drumbarr,
And flying on: I pictured what he told.

The crows that shake the night-damp off their wings
Upon the stones out yonder in the fields,
The first live things that we see in the mornings;
The crows that march across the fields, that sit
Upon the ash-trees' branches, that fly home
And crowd the elm-tops over in Drumbarr;
The crows we look on at all hours of light,
Growing, and full, and going—these black beings have
Another lifetime!

Crows flying in the dark—
Blackness in darkness flying; beings unseen

Except by eyes that are like to their own
Trespassers' eyes!

And you, old man, with eyes so quick and sharp,
Who've told me of the crows, my fosterer;
And you, old woman, upon whose lap I've lain
When I was taken from my mother's lap;
And you, young girl, with looks that have come down
From forefathers, my kin—ye have another life—
I've glimpsed it, I becoming trespasser—
Blackness in darkness flying like the crows!

IX

THERE is an hour, they say,
On which your dream has power;
Then all you wish for comes,
As comes the lost field-bird
Down to the island-lights;
There is an hour, they say,
That's woven with your wish:
In dawn, or dayli' gone,
In mirk-dark, or at noon,
In hush or hum of day,
May be that secret hour.

A herd-boy in the rain
Who looked o'er stony fields;
A young man in a street,
When fife and drum went by,
Making the sunlight shrill;
A girl in a lane,
When the long June twilight
Made friendly far-off things;
Had watch upon the hour;
The dooms they met are in
The song my grand-dam sings.

Circuit Five · The Town

I

THE stir of children with fresh dresses on,
And men who meet and say unguarded words,
And women from the coops
Of drudgeries removed,

And standing in this yard to watch come nigh.
Small pomps with pennons and with first spring flowers,
And, rosaries in hands,
Old women, three or four.

But he, when here he came, it was to front
Hard-handed men, and trouble them for dues—
Portion of what they ploughed
To stay the fatherless.

To win resource from them whose own resource
Was pittance—this he came here to do,
And gave for what he gained
His season of bright youth:

The hunt upon the mountain-side; the dance
Down in the vale; the whisper at the door;
Kiss on unstaying lips
That afterwards would stay;

Music he could have made would make our land
Of noble note and join our different breeds,
And make his name endeared
On roadside and in hall.

All this was changed, as when the warm stream
Setting through ocean towards vine-bearing isles,
Turns its flow towards capes
Where heather only thrives.

That day that was of battle and hard pledges
Has all been changed into this whitened morn—
Music and holiday,
And benediction bells;

With them outside who in dim corners sit,
Knitting or mending or with folded hands,—
Old women fingering o'er
Their old and heavy beads.

II

A BASKET-MAKER, an itinerant,
His hands as supple as the rods he bended:
I stayed to buy the withied shape he made.

And then a friend
Who had the lore of ancient fields and houses
Came to me there (it was a market-place).

Four arm-rings of gold
In box of alder-bark was in his gleanings
Where the receding lake had left behind
A bronze-age village; a quern in its place,
The grains it ground beside it—barley, wheat;
Two boar-tusk pendants and a piece of amber,
And under these, the woven hazel twigs
Laid down in summer, since the hazel nuts
Were not then filled; spindles and ox-yokes. . . .

I thought them apt, the woven hazel twigs
For there before us was a batch of them,
With rods that shone like amber—willow rods—
But they were not engaging to my friend:
He left me with the man of supple hands—
Two of us only in the market-place.

84

No tool he had but his own hands, a knife
That he had used since his apprenticeship
Which took him back, a youngster, by the pool
Where no one bided but the water-hen,
On in a dell when hazel-nuts were green,
And the wren showed the bulky nest he made
To his small mate. I watched him weave
Rod over rod, no gaps between the ridges.
And thought upon 'the woven hazel twigs
Laid down in summer, since the hazel nuts
Were not then ripe'. 'The basket on the arm
Of the old woman out for marketing;
The wicker round,' he said, 'the skib,
In which potatoes from the pot are poured;
The creel that brings the turf up from the bog;
The kish that holds them by the fireside:
There's no one marks them with a craftsman's name—
Scanted they are as commons of the house.'

And there it is—my thought came back to me!
You're one that's known
At doors, as is the thatcher or the weaver,
Or by the din you make, as the horse-shoer,
Before your name gets into household speech.
For if you find and bring material
From willow-pool or hazel-dell far-off,
And make a thing that is of shape and use
Without bystanders or the noise of tool,
You are not spoken of by man or woman.
'The basket-maker has no name,' he said.

But noteworthy! In Kerry glens, he told me,
Where grow the trees whose branches no one bends,

The old arbutus, the weavers' bundles
Are carried in his creels on asses' backs
Across the Reeks; the silver ring he showed me,
With two hands clasped, a Claddagh granny gave him
For baskets were a benefit to carry
Her fish to Galway in. And there he ended
His discourse and his task: he got his shillings
And I the withied shape was to my liking.

I watched him go, his stock-in-trade upon him.
'I travel Ireland's length and breadth,' he said.
There was dominion in the way he said it,
And in his even way towards other roofs,
A basket-maker, an itinerant.

III

THEY were hatched in the basket was under her bed,
And on her own floor
They were reared where she's seen them, between hob
     and threshold,
Between hearthstone and door!
And now to a market where prices are harried
Till they're nothing at all, the four ducks are carried!

And the time they's be gone her heart would be low,
And she'd murn an' murn,
And then they'd be back, and she'd hear in the lane
Their quack, quack of return;
And the cat would be vexed, and cross-eyed her looks
At the old body's joy when in came her ducks!

At noon they's be gone, but at dusk they'd be back
From the duck-pond in Urney,
And no hound would chase them that kept the good hours
On their back-and-forth journey;
No weasel nor wood-cat would near them and bite
An old body's ducks that were lucky and right!

From each end of the basket, too frightened to quack,
A duck sticks a beak,
And frightened is she, the old body who'd sell them,
And hardly will speak:
As she trudges along with her ducks, each as thin
As the water-hen!

I V

'I KNOW where I'd get
An ass that would do,
If I had the money—
A pound or two'—

Said a ragged man
To my uncle one day:
He got the money
And went on his way.

And after that time,
In market or fair
I'd look at the asses
That might be there,

And wonder what kind
Of an ass would do
For a ragged man
With a pound or two.

O, the black and roan horses the street would fill,
Their manes and tails streaming, and they standing still.

And their owners, the men of estate would be there,
Refusing gold guineas for a colt or a mare.

And one, maybe, riding up and down like a squire
So that buyers from Dublin might see and admire

The hunter or racer come to be sold
And be willing and ready to pay out their gold.

With men slouching beside them and buyers not near
It's no wonder the asses held down head and ear.

They had been sold and in by-ways bought
For a few half-crowns tied up in a knot,

And no one so poor as to buy one might come
To that fair that had horses so well prized at home!

> And then it fell out
> That at Arva or Scrabby,
> At some down-county fair,
> Or Mohill or Abbey,
>
> On two asses I happened—
> Without duress or dole
> They were there in the market
> A dam and her foal.
>
> And the owner, a woman,
> Did not slouch or stand,
> But in her cart sitting
> Was as grand as the grand;
>
> Like a queen out of Connacht
> From her toe to her tip,
> Like proud Granuaile
> On the deck of her ship.

And her hair—'twas a mane:
The blackberries growing
Out of the hedgerows
Have the sheen it was showing.

There kind was with kind
Like the flowers in the grasses—
If the owner was fine,
As fine were her asses.

White, white was the mother
As a dusty white road;
Black on back and on shoulders
The cross-marking showed.

She was tall—she could carry
A youth stout of limb,
Or bear down from the mountain
The bride decked for him!

Such was the mother—
The foal's hide was brown,
And fleecy and curly,
And soft like bog-down;

And it nuzzled its mother,
Its head to her knee,
And blue were its eyes
Like the pools of the sea!

Then I thought all the silver
My uncle could draw
Might not pay for the creatures
That that day I saw;

And I thought that old Damer,
Who had troughs made of gold,
Could not pay for the asses,
The young and the old.

And I think of them still
When I see on the roads
Asses unyoked
And asses with loads;

Or running and trotting,
With harness loose,
And a man striking and hitting
Where his stick has use;

And one with a hide
Like a patched-on sack
And two creels of turf
Upon its back;

And one in the market,
Meek and brown,
Its head to the cart-shafts
That are down;

Eating its forage—
A wisp of hay—
In the dust of the highway
Munching away;

Unmarked in the market
As might be a mouse
Behind a low stool
In a quiet house—

Then I think of the pair
Horses might not surpass—
The dam and her foal,
The white ass and brown ass.

V

'TIS long since, long since, since I heard
A tin-whistle played,
And heard the tunes, the ha'penny tunes
That nobody made!

The tunes that were before Cendfind
And Cir went Ireland's rounds—
That were before the surety
That strings have given sounds!

And now is standing in the mist,
And jigging backward there,
Shrilling with fingers and with breath,
A tin-whistle player!

He has hare's eyes, a long face rimmed
Around with badger-grey;
Aimless, like cries of mountain birds,
The tunes he has to play—

The tunes that are for stretches bare,
And men whose lives are lone—
And I had seen that face of his
Sculptured on cross of stone,
That long face, in a place of graves
With nettles overgrown.

VI

DOWN a street that once I lived in
You used to pass, a honey-seller,
And the town in which that street was
Was the shabbiest of all places:
You were different from the others
Who went by to barter meanly:
Different from the man with coloured
Windmills for the children's pennies;
Different from the drab purveyor
With her paper screens to fill up
Chill and empty fireplaces.

You went by, a man upstanding,
On your head a wide dish, holding
Dark and golden lumps of honey;
You went slowly, like an old horse
That's not driven any longer,
But that likes to take an amble.

No one ever bought your honey,
No one ever paid a penny
For a single comb of sweetness;
Every house was grim unto you
With foregone desire of eating
Bread whose taste had sweet of honey.

Yet you went, a man contented
As though you had a king to call on
Who would take you to his parlour,
And buy all your stock of honey.

On you went, and in a sounding
Voice, just like the bell of evening,
Told us of the goods you carried,
Told us of the dark and golden
Treasure dripping on your wide dish.

You went by, and no one named you!

VII

ONCE I loved a maiden fair,
Over the hills and far away,
Lands she had and lovers to spare,
Over the hills and far away.
And I was stooped and troubled sore,
And my face was pale, and the coat I wore
Was thin as my supper the night before,
Over the hills and far away.

Once I passed in the autumn late,
Over the hills and far away,
Her bawn and barn and painted gate,
Over the hills and far away.
She was leaning there in the twilight space,
Sweet sorrow was on her fair young face,
And her wistful eyes were away from the place,
Over the hills and far away.

Maybe she thought as she watched me come,
Over the hills and far away,
With my awkward stride and my face so glum,
Over the hills and far away.
Spite of his stoop, he still is young,
They say he goes the Shee* among,
Ballads he makes, I've heard them sung,
Over the hills and far away.

* Shee: *the fairies.*

93

She gave me good-night in gentle wise,
Over the hills and far away,
Shyly lifting to mine, dark eyes,
Over the hills and far away.
What could I do but stop and speak,
And she no longer proud, but meek?
She plucked me a rose like her wild-rose cheek—
Over the hills and far away.

Tomorrow, Mavourneen, a sleeveen* weds,
Over the hills and far away,
With corn in haggard and cattle in sheds,
Over the hills and far away.
And I who have lost her, the dear, the rare—
Well, I got me this ballad to sing at the fair,
'Twill bring enough money to drown my care,
Over the hills and far away.

* Sleeveen: *a sly fellow.*

VIII

THAT sidling creature is a little Fox:
Like other canines he is leashed and led;
Men trample; horses rear; he drags his leash.

Did not I
Once know a lad from Irrus where they leave
Mittens for foxes; where they invite
A fox to a child's christening; where they have
Foxes as gossips to their boys and girls?

Would that the lad from Irrus now was here
To tell his gossip that a human creature
Has heart for him, and fain would cover up
His bowels of dread, and find some way to bring
His rainy hills around him, the soft grass,
Darkness of ragged hedges, and his earth—
The black, damp earth under the roots of trees!
Would that the lad from Irrus now was here
Where houses tower and where horses rear!

IX

MEET for a town where pennies have few pairs
In children's pockets, this toy-shop with its wares—
Jews' harps and masks and kites,
And paper lanterns with their farthing lights,
All in a dim-lit window to be seen:
Within—
The walls that have the patches of the damp,
The counter where there burns the murky lamp,
And there, the counter and the shelf between
The dame,
Meagre, grey-polled, lame.

And here she's been since times are legendary,
For Miler Dowdall whom we used to see
Upon the billboards with deft hands held up
To win the champion's belt or silver cup,
Would come in here to buy a kite or top—
That Miler Dowdall, the great pugilist
Who had the world once beneath his fist—
Now Miler's is a name that's blown by!

How's custom? Bad enough! She had not sold
More than a dozen kites for boys to hold—
She sold them by the gross in times a-gone;
Wasn't it poor, the town
Where little girls could not spend on a doll,
Nor boys on marbles or on tops at all?
And toys!
The liveliest were stiffened like herself,
The brightest grown drab upon the shelf!

But she's not tragical—no, not a whit:
She laughs as she talks to you—that is it—
As paper-lantern with its farthing light
Her eyes are bright;
And as a kite held by a string that's worn,
Her spare, lame frame's upborne,
And like a Jew's harp when you strike its tongue—
That way her voice goes on and on and she will hop
The inches of her crib, this narrow shop.
When you step in to be her customer:
A bird of little worth, a sparrow, say,
Whose crib's in some neglected passageway,
That one's left wondering who brings crumbs to her.

How strange to think that she is still inside
After so many turns to the tide—
Since this lit window was a dragon's eye
To turn us all to wonder coming nigh—
Since this dim window was a dragon's eye!

X

My young love said to me, 'My brothers won't mind,
And my parents won't slight you for your lack of kind.'
Then she stepped away from me, and this she did say,
'It will not be long, love, till our wedding day.'

She stepped away from me and she moved through the fair,
And fondly I watched her go here and go there,
Then she went her way homeward with one star awake,
As the swan in the evening moves over the lake.

The people were saying no two were e'er wed
But one had a sorrow that never was said,
And I smiled as she passed with her goods and her gear,
And that was the last that I saw of my dear.

I dreamt it last night that my young love came in,
So softly she entered, her feet made no din;
She came close beside me, and this she did say,
'It will not be long, love, till our wedding day.'

Circuit Six · Women in the House

I

A DAY of distant reverence—
Saint Anne's feast day it was:
The shadow on the right, my size,
Went along the grass

As far as to the blackthorn hedge,
The boundary to the scythe,
Where violets have leave to grow
With mosses underneath.

And there, to greet me on her porch
Where woodbine ivies met,
Brown-eyed, with blessing in her speech,
My aunt Margaret!

Changed, changed, the countryside, all changed!
Kindred and household gone,
And weathered now their histories
As slabs of churchyard stone!

But still there is remembrance—
Lightly I wrote those lines,
Not knowing that remembrance
Had reached into my veins!

And ordained so I make my way
To thresholds I have known,
And see, each one with her own look,
Rose, Maurya, Anne, Shevaun.

And in their own, their living voice,
A history I hear,
And make the most of what they tell—
Maid, wife, or grandmother.

II

FOR a bride you have come! Is it with a full score
Of rake-hell rapscallions you'd fill up my door,
With a drum to your tail and a fiddle before,
And a bag-piper playing all through ye?

My faith! Do you think that a shy little maid
Would lift up her head before such a brigade,
When an arm round her waist would make her afraid?
By my hand! She has gone from my keeping.

Through the gap in the hedges away she has run;
Like the partridge across the wide stubble she's gone,
And here I am, here I am, here I'm alone
With no daughter to give any comer!

Well, here she is back! I declare she has come
Like the cat to the cradle, and Nance she's at home:
O my love, would you go to the bleak hills of Crome,
Where nor manners nor mirth are in fashion?

O say not you'll go! That you'll never embark
From a plentiful house where you prize every spark,
Where there's milk in the crock and meal in the ark,
And a pair of fat ducks for the roasting!

Oh, mother sell all that you have to your name,
To give me a dowry to equal my fame—
Sell the cow, and the sow, and the gander that's lame,
And the sack of black wool in the corner!

And my good-will I'll leave to our Babe that stays here,
May she leave the bog-bottoms within the half-year,
Where the rushes are high and the curlews call near,
And the crows on the hills they are lonely.

With rake-hell young fellows my Babe will not go,
Nor look from her dormer on faction below,
From up where the picture and looking-glass show
That elegance holds and good order!

III

A young girl sings:

The Lannan Shee*
Watched the young man Brian
Cross over the stile towards his father's door,
And she said, 'No help,
For now he'll see
His byre, his bawn, and his threshing-floor!
And, oh, the swallows
Forget all wonders
When walls with the nests rise up once more!'
    My strand is knit.

'Out of the dream
Of me, into
The round of his labour he will grow;
To spread his fields
In the winds of spring,
And tramp the heavy glebe and sow;
And cut and clamp
And rear the turf
Until the season when they mow.'
    My wheel runs smooth.

* The Lannan Shee: *The Fairy Sweetheart.*

'And while he toils
In field and bog
He will be anxious in his mind
About the thatch
Of barn and rick
Against the reiving autumn wind,
And how to make
His gap and gate
Secure against the thieving kind.'
    My wool is fine.

'He has gone back;
No more I'll see
Mine image in his deepening eyes;
Then I'll lean above
The Well of the Bride,
And with my beauty, peace will rise !
O autumn star
In a lake well hid,
Fill up my heart and make me wise !'
    My quick brown wheel.

'The women bring
Their pitchers here
At the time when the stir of the house is o'er;
They'll see my face
In the well-water,
And they'll never lift their pitchers more.
For each will say
"How beautiful—
Why should I labour any more?
Indeed I come
Of a race so fine
'Twere waste to labour any more !"'
    My thread is spun.

Another girl sings:

One came before her and said, beseeching,
'I have fortune and I have lands,
And if you'll share in the goods of my household
All my treasure's at your commands.'

But she said to him, 'The goods you proffer
Are far from my mind as the silk of the sea!
The arms of him, my young love, round me
Is all the treasure that's true for me!'

'Proud you are then, proud of your beauty,
But beauty's a flower will soon decay;
The fairest flowers they bloom in the summer
They bloom one summer, and they fade away.'

'My heart is sad, then, for the little flower
That must so wither where fair it grew—
He who has my heart in keeping,
I would he had my body too.'

An old woman sings:

There was an oul' trooper went riding by
On the road to Carricknabauna,
And the sorrow is better to sing than cry
On the way to Carricknabauna!
And as this oul' trooper went riding on
He heard this sung by a crone, a crone,
On the road to Carricknabauna!

'I'd spread my cloak for you, young lad,
Were it only the breadth of a farthen,
And if your mind was as good as your work,
In troth, it's you I'd rather!

In dread of e'er forgetting this,
And before we go any farther,
Hoist me up to the top of the hill,
And show me Carricknabauna!

'Carricknabauna, Carricknabauna,
Would you show me Carricknabauna?
I lost a horse at Cruckmoylinn,
At the Cross of Bunratty I dropped a limb,
But I left my youth beyond on the hill,
Over at Carricknabauna!'

IV

THE fiddles were playing and playing,
The couples were out on the floor;
From converse and dancing he drew me,
And across the door.

Ah! strange were the dim, wide meadows,
And strange was the cloud-strewn sky,
And strange in the meadows the corncrakes,
And they making cry!

The hawthorn bloom was by us,
Around us the breath of the south—
White hawthorn, strange in the night-time—
His kiss on my mouth!

V

O MEN from the fields!
Come gently within.
Tread softly, softly,
O men coming in!

Mavourneen is going
From me and from you,
Where Mary will fold him
With mantle of blue!

From reek of the smoke
And cold of the floor,
And the peering of things
Across the half-door.

O men from the fields!
Soft, softly come through—
Mary puts round him
Her mantle of blue.

V I

I HEARD in the night the pigeons
Stirring within their nest:
The wild pigeons' stir was tender,
Like a child's hand at the breast.

I cried, 'O stir no more!
(My breast was touched with tears)
O pigeons, make no stir—
A childless woman hears.'

VII

ONE day you'll come to my husband's door,
  Dermott Donn MacMorna,
One day you'll come to Hugh's dark door,
And the pain at my heart will be no more,
  Dermott Donn MacMorna!

From his bed, from his fire I'll rise,
  Dermott Donn MacMorna,
From the bed of Hugh, from his fire I'll rise,
With my laugh for the pious, the quiet, the wise,
  Dermott Donn MacMorna!

Lonesome, lonesome, the house of Hugh,
  Dermott Donn MacMorna,
No cradle rocks in the house of Hugh;
The listening fire has thought of you,
  Dermott Donn MacMorna!

Out of this loneliness we'll go,
  Dermott Donn MacMorna,
Together at last we two will go
Down a darkening road with a gleam below.
Ah, but the winds do bitter blow,
  Dermott Donn MacMorna!

VIII

THE little moths are creeping
Across the cottage pane;
On the floor the chickens gather,
And they make talk and complain.

And she sits by the fire
Who has reared so many men;
Her voice is low like the chickens'
With the things she says again:

'The sons that come back do be restless,
They search for the thing to say;
Then they take thought like the swallows,
And the morrow brings them away.

In the old, old days upon Innish,
The fields were lucky and bright,
And if you lay down you'd be covered
By the grass of one soft night.

And doves flew with every burial
That went from Innishore—
Two white doves before the coffined—
But the doves fly no more!'

She speaks and the chickens gather,
And they make talk and complain,
While the little moths are creeping
Across the cottage pane.

IX

OH, to have a little house!
To own the hearth and stool and all!
The heaped-up sods upon the fire,
The pile of turf against the wall!

To have a clock with weights and chains
And pendulum swinging up and down,
A dresser filled with shining delph,
Speckled and white and blue and brown!

I could be busy all the day
Clearing and sweeping hearth and floor,
And fixing on their shelf again
My white and blue and speckled store!

I could be quiet there at night
Beside the fire and by myself,
Sure of a bed and loth to leave
The ticking clock and the shining delph!

Och! but I'm weary of mist and dark,
And roads where there's never a house nor bush,
And tired I am of bog and road,
And the crying wind and the lonesome hush!

And I am praying to God on high,
And I am praying him night and day,
For a little house, a house of my own—
Out of the wind's and the rain's way.

X

THE Mountain Thrush I say,
But I am thinking of her, Nell the Rambler:
She'd come down to our houses bird-alone,
From some haunt that was hers, and we would see her
Drawing the water from the well one day,
For one house or another, or we'd hear her
Garrulous with the turkeys down the street,
We children.

From neighbour's house to neighbour's house she'd go
Until one day we'd see
Her worn cloak hanging behind our door;
And then, that night, we'd hear
Of Earl Gerald: how he rides abroad,
His horse's hooves shod with the weighty silver,
And how he'll ride all roads till those silver shoes
Are worn thin;
As thin as the cat's ears before the fire,
Upraised in such content before the fire,
And making little lanterns in the firelight.

The Mountain Thrush, when every way's a hard one,
Hops on in numbness till a patch of sunlight,
Falling, will turn her to a wayside song;
So it was with her, Rambler Nell, a shelter,
A bit upon the board, and she flowed on
With rambler's discourse—tales, and rhymes, and sayings,
With child's light in her worn eyes, and laughter
To all her words.

The lore she had—
'Twas like a kingly robe, on which long rains
Have fallen and fallen, and parted
The finely woven web, and have washed away
The kingly colours, but have left some threads
Still golden, and some feathers still as shining
As the kingfisher's. While she sat there, not spinning,
Not weaving anything but her own fancies,
We ate potatoes out of the ash, and thought them
Like golden apples out of Tiprobane.

When winter's over-long, and days that famish
Come one upon another like snowflakes,
The Mountain Thrush makes way down to our houses:
Hops round for crumbs, and stays a while, a comer
Upon our floors.

She did not think
Bread of dependence bitter; three went with her—
Hunger, Sorrow, and Loneliness—and they
Had crushed all that makes claims, though they'd not bent her,
Nor emptied her of trust—what was it led her
From house to house, but that she always looked for
A warmer welcome at the hearth ahead?

So she went on until it came one day,
The Mountain Thrush's heart-stop on the way.

XI

THE hawthorn now
Is gone from the hedge,
But a moon-coloured spray,
And a foam-coloured spray
Are near the thatch,

Where, round the porch
With stem as thick
As beam within,
The woodbine grows.

The ash tree planted
With the same spade
Is neighbour only;
Geraniums set
On window-sill
Last but as long
As the red paint
Or whitewash coat
On door, on wall;
Nothing that grows
Is leased so long,
So close to the house
As this hedgeling.

Our *Póisín glégeal**
Finds fragrance nigh her,
And, ere she raises
The latch to bring her
To dance within—
The moon-coloured spray,
The foam-coloured spray
Is at her breast.
With scent of that
Which bides by the house,
So long, so close,
The hedgerow bloom!

* Póisín glégeal: *little bright flower; a name of endearment given to a young girl.*

113

Circuit Seven · People on the Road

I

Spadesman:

It is but seldom that we Spadesmen have
A Scholar with us when we're on the mission—
Well, maybe, never. Here's where one of us
Spies a field where spade is likely needed
And leaves our rank. Days are all they'll give him.

Scholar:

You are alert for what the farmer's book
Has printed for you.

Spadesman:

We're farmers' sons, boys of the little patch—
We go towards where domains are. We know the fields.
And they are tinkers on the other side.
They have no friendliness for field or house.
They have a curse for all who own a roof:
I heard one say it:

> You build houses—Aye, like the crows you put stick
> and stick together.
> May I see a scatter of sticks and the kites a-chase in the
> wood!
> You live man and wife, you say! Like the goats, two
> and two a-tether,
> For fear you would reach to the hedge-top and the wild
> taste get in your blood!

Scholar:

The tinkers! They are vagrants born and bred.
But there are others not tied to a place
You pass the time of day with.

Spadesman:

Oh, there are,
You'll meet a score of such in a day's walk—
Men and women of no fixed abode
As papers say, but with no venom in them.

Scholar:

The spades you shoulder have a glint in them—
What forge did they come out of?

Spadesman:

The blacksmith's—
Like horses' shoes, or asses' shoes, or like
The crook that hangs the pot above the fire.

Scholar:

The blacksmiths make you spades now, but I've heard
The whitesmiths made them once.

Spadesman:

That's handed down:
I've heard old men colloguing in a forge
When sledge was laid, about the olden times
When spades were made—no, not for every toiler
That broke a ridge, but for the rambling spadesmen—
By the whitesmiths.

Scholar:

They had a name—
The men who shouldered spades along old roads:
They left a legend, or, maybe, they took
A legend over.

Spadesman:

Swords were forged
Not by the blacksmiths, I heard old men say,
But by the whitesmiths, and when swordsmen went
Across the seas, the whitesmiths put
Their art into the making of the spades
Shouldered and used by men the like of us.

Scholar:

They were the last blades that our whitesmiths tempered—
Valour was in them, and, I deem, a portion
Of fame of those who wielded their broadswords
At Limerick and Clonmel! They flashed, I warrant,
On spadesmens' shoulders, going the old roads!

Spadesman:

But they were used as any other spades,
I'd have you know, to dig and delve for hours.

Scholar:

A poet shouldered spade that could have been
The whitesmith's work, Owen Roe O'Sullivan.
And ere the steward came to count the ridges
He and his comrades dug, he could recite
To ragged or to frieze-clad men the story
Of field where princes fell (spades in the mould!),
And Hector's gleaming blade (the steward's shout!).

Spadesman:

'Twas long day's digging, and by rain-drenched men,
Or sweating men, and at the end of it,
The men could sleep on harrows, I'll be bound,
Or on whin-bushes, no matter whether spades
They used were blacksmiths' or whitesmiths' finding.
And here's the cross-roads; you'll meet others now,
The men and women seasoned for the roads.

II

SOJOURNER, set down
Your skimming wheel;
Nothing is sharp
That we have of steel:
Nothing has edge—
Oh, whirl around
Your wheel of stone
Till our blades be ground!

Harshly, quickly, under blades
Hafted with horn and wood and bone,
Went the wheel:
Narrow long knives that should be one edge,
House-knives that sliced the loaf to the heel,
And scraped scales off mackerel,
And weighty knives that were shaped like a wedge—
Stone wakened keenness in their steel:
Knives with which besom-makers pare
Their heather-stalks, and hawkers' blades
Used by men of a dozen trades:
Broad-bladed knives that cut bacon-sides,
And stumpy knives for cobblers' hides,
With hunters' knives that were thinned with wear:
All were brought to,
All were laid on,
All were ground by
The Sojourner's wheel.

And those who filled the market-square
Saw hand and eye upon their ware
That were well schooled and scrupulous
To spend upon that task their use.

But sparks came from the eyes and met
The sparks that were from the edges whet,
As eagerly and wittingly
The dullness of each blade scoured he,
And the brow he bent was like a stone.

Over the grinding-stone he sang,
'The dalesman's sword shall make you fear,
And the dirk in the grasp of the mountaineer,
And likewise the pirate's blue cutlass
Who have left your blades long edgeless!'
But the men were thinking of games of cards,
And the looks of the boys were turned towards
The corner where they played pitch and toss,
And the women thought of the herring across
The tongs to roast where pot-hooks hang.

'Unready and unforward men
Who have no right to any lien
On the gifts of Tubal Cain,
The gifts of our father, Tubal Cain!'

But no one drew meaning from the song
As he made an equal edge along
One side of the blade and the other one,
And polished the surface till it shone.

'Now leave a blessing on what you have done.'

'For what I have done I take my feel,
But no blessing I leave on it,' said he.
'Everybody knows,
Everybody knows
That the knife-grinder
No blessing bestows.'

Then the market-place, with wheel a-pack,
He left, and the men to their cards went back
And talked of a bird in the cocker's loft;
And of liming linnets beside the croft
The boys told between pitch and toss;
And the women laid the herring across
The tongs to roast for a sloven's meal.

And he went out beside the Peel
Tower, and through Saint Selskar's Gate,
Heading at a hearty rate
Towards the hilltops and the shades.

And three who brought back sharpened blades
To their fathers' stalls by the Tan-yard Side,
And then stayed while a blackbird cried
Quietly by their groundsills—
The butcher's daughter,
The cobbler's daughter,
The hawker's daughter,
Were lost on the hills!

III

A HUNDRED men think I am theirs when with them I drink ale,
But their presence fades away from me and their high spirits fail
When I think upon your converse kind by the meadow and the
        linn,
And your form smoother than the silk on the Mountain of
        O'Flynn.

Oh, Pauric, is it pain to you that I'm wasting night and day,
And, Pauric, is it grief to you that I'll soon be in the clay?
My first love with the winning mouth, my treasure you'll abide,
Till the narrow coffin closes me and the grass grows through my
        side.

The man who strains to leap the wall, we think him foolish still,
When to his hand is the easy ditch to vault across at will;
The rowan tree is fine and high, but bitter its berries grow,
While blackberries and raspberries are on shrubs that blossom
low.

Farewell, farewell, forever, to yon town amongst the trees;
Farewell, the town that draws me on mornings and on eves.
Oh, many's the ugly morass now, and many's the crooked road
That lie henceforth between me and where my heart's bestowed.

And Mary, Ever Virgin, where will I turn my head!
I know not where his house is built, nor where his fields are
spread.
Ah, kindly was the counsel that my kinsfolk gave to me,
'The hundred twists are in his heart, and the thousand tricks
has he.'

IV

NOR right, nor left, nor any road I see a comrade's face,
Nor word to lift the heart in me I hear in any place;
They leave me, who pass by me, to my loneliness and care,
Without a house to draw my step nor a fire that I might share.

Ochone, before our people knew the scatt'ring of the dearth,
Before they saw potatoes rot and melt black in the earth,
I might have stood in Connacht, on the top of Cruckmaelinn,
And all around me I would see the hundreds of my kin.

V

MAVOURNEEN, we'll go far away
From the net of the crooked town
Where they grudge us the light of the day.

Around my neck you will lay
Two tight little arms of brown.
 Mavourneen, we'll go far away
 From the net of the crooked town.

And what will we hear on the way?
The stir of wings up and down
In nests where the little birds stay!
 Mavourneen, we'll go far away
 From the net of the crooked town
 Where they grudge us the light of the day.

VI

I AM the Toy-maker; I have brought from the town
As much in my pack as should fetch a whole crown,
I'll array for you now my stock of renown,
And many's the raree will show you.

Here's a horse that is rearing to bound through the smoke
Of cannon and musket, and, face to that ruck,
The horseman with sword ready held for the stroke,
Lord Lucan, maybe, or Prince Charlie.

An old woman sitting and waiting for call,
With her baskets of cockles and apples and all;
A one-legged sailor attending a ball,
And a tailor and nailer busy.

Or would you have these? A goose ganging by,
With head up in challenge to all who come nigh;
A cock with a comb dangling over his eye,
And a hen on a clutch nicely sitting;

Or a duck that is chasing a quick thing around,
Or a crow that is taking three hops on the ground,
Or an ass with head down (he is held in a pound),
Or a fox with tail curled around him?

A ship made of shells that have sheen on the sea,
All ready to sail for black Barbarie,
The Lowlands of Holland, or High Germanie—
And who'll be the one that will steer her?

I'll speak of my trade: there's a day beyond day
When the hound needn't hunt and the priest needn't pray,
And the clerk needn't write, and the hen needn't lay,
Whence come all the things that I show you.

I am the Toy-maker; upon the town wall
My crib is high up; I have down-look on all,
And coach and wheelbarrow I carve in my stall,
Making things with no troubles in them.

VII

You blew in
Where Jillin Brady kept up state on nothing,
Married her daughter, and brought to Jillin's house
A leash of dogs, a run of ferrets, a kite
In a wired box; linnets and larks and goldfinches
In their proper cages; and you brought with you this song:

If you come to look for me,
Perhaps you'll not me find:
For I'll not in my Castle be—
Inquire where horns wind.

Before I had a man-at-arms
I had an eager hound:
Then was I known as Reynardine,
In no crib to be found.

You used to say
Five hounds' lives were a man's life, and when Teague
Had died of old age, and when Fury that was a pup
When Teague was maundering, had turned from hill to hearth
And lay in the dimness of a hound's old age,
I went with you again, and you were upright
As the circus-rider standing on his horse;
Quick as a goat that will take any path, and lean—
Lean as a lash; you'd have no speech
With wife or child or mother-in-law till you
Were out of doors and standing on the ditch,
Ready to face the river or the hill:

The Hen-wife's son once heard the grouse
Talk to his soft-voiced mate;
And what he heard the heath-poult say
The loon would not relate.

Impatient in the yard he grew,
And patient on the hill;
Of cocks and hens he'd take no charge,
And he went with Reynardine.

Lean days when we were idle as the birds,
That will not preen their feathers, but will travel
To taste a berry, or pull a shred of wool
That they will never use. We pass the bound:
A forest's grave, the black bog is before us,
And in its very middle you will show me
The snipe's nest that is lonelier than the snipe
That's all that's there; and then a stony hill,
A red fox climbing, pausing, looking round his tail
At us travailing against wind and rain
To reach the river-spring where Finn or Fergus
Hardened a spear, back of a thousand years.

And still your cronies are what they were then—
The hounds that know the hill and know the hearth
(One is Fury that's as old as Argos now
That crawled to Odysseus coming back);
Your minstrels, the blackbird singing still
When kites are leaving, crows are going home,
And the thrush in the morning like a spectre showing
Beside the day-spring; and your visitors,
The cuckoo that will swing upon a branch,
The corncrake with quick head between the grass-tufts.
And still your song is what it used to be—
About that Reynardine who came to lord
A castle (O that castle with its trees!),
Who heard the horns, and let his turret grow
The foxglove where his banner should be seen:

        The hawk is for the hill, he cried,
        The badger for the glen;
        The otter for the river-pools—
        Amen, amen, amen!

VIII

I WENT out in the evening, my sweetheart for to find;
I stood by her cottage window, as well I do mind;
I stood by her cottage window, and I thought I would get in,
But instead of pleasures for me my sorrows did begin!

Fine colour had my darling though it wasn't me was there:
I did not sit beside her, but inside there was a pair!
I stood outside the window like a poor neglected soul,
And I waited till my own name was brought across the coal!

Here's a health unto the blackbird that sings upon the tree,
And here's to the willy wagtail that goes the road with me!
Here's a health unto my darling and to them she makes her own:
She's deserving of good company; for me, I go my lone.

My love she is courteous and handsome and tall;
For wit and behaviour she's foremost of them all!
She says she is in no way bound, that with me she'll go free,
But my love has too many lovers to have any love for me!

IX

THAT star I know is Betelgeux:
But when I climb the hill by day
His splendid name I hardly ken—
He is star-marches far away.

Then when at night I travel on,
Wide-wakeful in an empty land,
Than Betelgeux, my star of stars,
No living thing is nearer hand.

So send a ray that I may own
The fortune that is mine,
O Betelgeux you princely star,
My forehead's for your shine.

Until, days, nights gone, in a stream I see
You pulse from marge to main,
And know what dust my bone and flesh will be
Ere you pulse there again!

Circuit Eight · Monuments

I

Maurice:

And we are here to look into a house
Where there's not even a forgotten stool,
You at the doorway, I where the window was.
I see the broken hearthstone.

Terence:

A patch of sunlight on the crumbled wall!
A loom was there; it was a young girl's own.

Maurice:

       Yes, where the window was.
And all around us are the places named
In legend while the pot boiled on the hearth—
Urney and Kevitt and Cullismore,
Famous for bluebells, nut-dells, an old rath,
Or ditches where the whins had brighter gold.

Terence:

The clatter of the house gone with the smoke
Of peats new laid around the morning fire,
And burning rightly, brightly, quietly—
Clack of the loom was all the outer sound—
A beat, a measure of accord between
Her mind and loom, the shuttles and her hand.
It was a yard-long loom and framed for her
By an old uncle, a thoughtful man
Who kept in trim a dozen beds of flowers
Behind a fuchsia hedge. My thread is weak
To cross to who he was or where he was,
But she sat there, young mistress of the loom
And wove the grey or brown and therewith dreamed
More glowing patterns in the days to be.

Maurice:

A change as great as any were foretold
In Columbkill's quaint prophecies is here—
Carriages without horses, and the hound
The calf displacing in the favoured nook.
A broken quern-stone once held that gate:
A man from the Museum was searching for it,
But where it's gone there's nobody can tell.

Terence:

This was the time when she was most herself:
She'd run to neighbours' houses, offer them
The things she wove, and brighter things than webs,
Things that she made with feathers and with flowers.
Like the wren's bevy ravelled from the nest,
Where no one knows they're gone.

Maurice:

But like the sun upon a patch of sail
Of vessel long delayed, the prophecy
Fulfilled, of the old stock restored,
And names contemned now honoured to the full.

Terence:

Now that her grand-daughter has come to wed
(She has the bright hair and the pointed face
That made the older kindred so remarked
By those who kept in mind the lineages)
She is bethought on. The time is when
The blackthorn's faint bloom is on the hedge.

Maurice:

What would you have fulfilled
For those who come into the after-story?

Terence:

Bread eaten without debt to harden it,
Space in a house, no cark to waken to,
And no word said that brings an inner moan
And not a faithful answer; over these,
Work of the day that brings enough to keep
Brave an innocence in its walks and ways,
And festivals from time to time that mean
A share in revelry or in devotion,
And friends to take one out of the four walls
To some enjoyment that is like a ransom.

Maurice:

And so we turn from window-sill and door
Now that we only speak in prophecies.

Terence (as they go on):

I'll turn the prophecies. The mound that's yonder—
A thousand years ago men looked towards it,
And named the kingly men who had possessed
Its ramparts, with regret for shortened days.
I know the old poem that recounts the kings.

> The fort over against the oak-wood—
> It was Bruidge's, it was Cathal's,
> It was Aed's, it was Ailill's,
> It was Conaing's, it was Cuilíne's,
> It was Maeldúin's.
> The fort remains after each in his turn,
> And the kings asleep in the ground! *

Maurice:

The great house that was built on a domain
Forfeited from one who thought the Stuart
Was rightful king, is gone to wrack and ruin.
The castle and the cashel, too, are empty.

* *This verse was translated by Kuno Meyer.*

Terence:

And back a thousand years before the mound—
The cromlech—one great stone upon two uprights.
Men looked upon it and had grief to think
That so much power was covered by the stones.

Maurice:

We'd see in every age if we went back,
Some heritage destroyed or else forsaken,
And we would know how change makes way for change.

II

THE Blackbird of Litir Lone
That pensive Finn famed so,
The thrush that in the evening sang
Ar bhán chnuic Eireann—O!

Where have they gone and left our woods
And fields without a note
Except the ground tone of the rooks
Gathered from their rout?

The simple fields now make their own
Of the unuséd light;
More than the hedge, the ivy crop
On ruined wall is bright;

And now the grass-tufts take the glow,
The thorn bush is revealed
A relic of the ancientry
The rath has left the field;

And Katie on her doorstep stands
Withheld; she would call in
The errant clutch the yellow hen
Has hatched out in the whin.

But no bird sings from thorn bush,
From hedge or leafy sill—
Where have they gone, the speckled breast,
And where, the yellow bill?

What grim marauder made a spoil
Of bird and nestling,
And left to us the songless woods,
The songless fields of Eirinn?

III

An old man said, 'I saw
The chief of the things that are gone;
A stag with head held high,
A doe, and a fawn;

And they were the deer of Ireland
That scorned to breed within bound:
The last; they left no race
Tame on a pleasure-ground.

A stag, with his hide all rough
With the dew, and a doe and a fawn;
Nearby, on their track on the mountain,
I watched them, two and one,

Down to the Shannon going—
Did its waters cease to flow
When they passed, they that carried the swiftness
And the pride of long ago?

The last of the troop that had heard
Finn's and Oscar's cry;
A doe and a fawn, and before,
A stag with head held high!'

IV

THE crows still fly to that wood, and out of the wood she comes,
Carrying her load of sticks, a little less now than before,
Her strength being less; she bends as the hoar rush bends in the
    wind;
She will sit by the fire, in the smoke, her thoughts on root and the
    living branch no more.

The crows still fly to that wood, that wood that is sparse and
    gapped;
The last one left of the herd makes way by the lane to the stall,
Lowing distress as she goes; the great trees there are all down;
No fiddle sounds in the hut tonight, and a candle only gives light
    to the hall.

The trees are gapped and sparse, yet a sapling spreads on the joints
Of the wall, till the castle stones fall down into the moat:
The last one who minds that our race once stood as a spreading
    tree,
She goes, and thorns are bare, where the blackbird, his summer
    songs done, strikes one metal note.

V

'A STRANGER you came to me over the Sea,
But welcome I made you, Seamus-a-ree,
And shelter I gave you, my sons set to ward you,
Red war I faced for you, Seamus-a-ree.*

Now a craven you go from me over the Sea,
But my best sons go with you, Seamus-a-ree;
Foreign graves they will gain, and for those who remain
The black hemp is sown—och, Seamus-a-ree!

    * Seamus-a-ree: *James the King—James II.*

But the Boyne shall flow back from the wide Irish Sea,
On the Causeway of Aughrim our victory shall be:
Two hundreds of years and the child on the knee
Will be rocked to this cronach, Seamus-a-ree!'

VI

ERE Titan his limbs from the clouds had divested
I strayed to the top of a hill in the North,
And there I beheld—O moment restoring!
The three bright-faced girls from Finvarra's Court.

A mist was resplendent—from the cairns of Galway
To the invers* of Cork it sparkled and shone;
Arbutus and apple were on the tree branches
And honey dripped down to the edge of the stone.

Each lighted a flambeau—Fand, Cleena, and Aunya;
I followed the band up hill and through glade,
I asked what appointment had brought them amongst us,
And why was the progress so royally made?

As the sound of a bell one hears of a sudden,
The answer rang through me—'the flambeaux are lit
For sake of the King who is now bound for Eirinn,
Who to Justice and Faith the Three Kingdoms will knit!'

As the sound of a bell, though the ringing be over,
Stays on in the hearing, their tone stirred the air,
As I wandered alone on the ground that was greening,
Without stress, without pain, without bondage to care.

What was lost was restored, what was empty replenished,
And term was set to the wrong we resisted;
But I looked in the gloom and was prone and defeated
Ere Titan his limbs from the clouds had divested!

* Invers: *inlets.*

139

VII

SHALL I go bound and you go free,
And love one so removed from me?
Not so! The falcon o'er my brow
Hath better quest I dare avow.

And must I run where you will ride,
And must I stay where you abide?
Not so! The feather that I wear
Is from an eyrie in the air.

And must I climb a broken stair,
And must I pace a chamber bare?
Not so! The Brenny plain is wide
And there are banners where I ride.

And other speech than this I chose
To charm your ear, my English rose!
The word has come from great O'Neill—
The blade I bear is Spanish steel.

VIII

O WOMAN, shapely as the swan,
On your account I shall not die:
The men you've slain—a trivial clan—
Were less than I.

I ask me shall I die for these—
For blossom teeth and scarlet lips—
And shall that delicate swan-shape
Bring me eclipse?

140

Well-shaped the breasts and smooth the skin,
The cheeks are fair, the tresses free—
And yet I shall not suffer death,
God over me!

Those even brows, that hair like gold,
Those languorous tones, that virgin way,
The flowing limbs, the rounded heel
Slight men betray!

Thy spirit keen through radiant mien,
Thy shining throat and smiling eye,
Thy little palm, thy side like foam—
I cannot die!

O woman shapely as the swan,
In a cunning house hard-reared was I:
O bosom white, O well-shaped palm,
I shall not die!

IX

NOT as a woman of the English weeping over a lord of the
    English
Do I weep—
A cry that scarcely stirs the heart!
I lament as it is in my blood to lament—
Castle and stronghold are broken,
And the sovereign of the land beside the lake lies dead—
Mahon O'Reilly!
In his day the English were broken:
I weep beside Loch Sheelin and the day is long and grey!

X

HERE, as a bare, unlichened wall, the castle front goes up,
But empty inside, empty all, as empty as a cup
A laggard left within the breach after the last sup.

But horses glistened in the court, the breed of Saladin,
And falcons from MacMurrough's perch looked round with
     baleful eyne;
The Statutes of FitzEmpress were held by aureate men.

I look to where the apertures, one over one, make space
Within the massiveness of wall: such blue there never was!
Never in any place, I say, was such translucent glass!

And then the thought: how ignorant! No window pane was set
Within the depth of loop-hole that I am gazing at,
Making scrutable the figured cloth where prancing beast meets
     scathe.

And thereupon entrancement grew: deep, clear, unearthly
As syllables in holy words the blue was lined on high:
At Ferns Castle yesterday I looked upon the sky!

XI

ABOVE me stand, worn from their ancient use,
The King's, the Bishop's, and the Warrior's house,
Quiet as folds upon a grassy knoll:
Stark-grey they stand, wall joined to ancient wall,
Chapel, and Castle, and Cathedral.

It is not they are old, but stone by stone
Into another lifetime they have grown,
The life of memories an old man has:
They dream upon what things have come to pass,
And know that stones grow friendly with the grass.

The name has crumbled—CASHEL that has come
From conqueror-challenging CASTELLUM—
Walls in a name ! No citadel is here,
Now as a fane the empty walls uprear
Where green and greener grass spreads far and near !

XII

IT would not be far for us two to go back to the Age of Bronze:
This mound was your father's dún, and here he ruled as a King,
With herd of horses, good tilth upon the face of four hills,
And clumps of cattle beyond them where rough-browed men
  showed spears.

How fair you were when you walked beside the old forest trees !
So fair that I thought you were her whom Fergus wooed for his
  love—
Flidais the forest queen, to whom no trampling of herds,
No roar of contending bulls came through in her hidden glades.

I called three times as an owl; through the gap where the herders
  watched
You ran, and we climbed the heights where the brackens pushed
  at our knees,
And we lay where the brackens drew the earth-smell out of the
  earth,
And journeyed and baffled the fighters of three ill-wishing kings.

It would not be far for us two to go back to the Age of Bronze:
The fire the nomads left is lone as a burning ship;
We eat them as we pass by, sweet ears of the green wheat,
And come to the dún again when your father's rule was bygone.

And the peace that I made by my rule was whole as a frozen well,
And my name was borne as far as to where the amber lies:
The rule and the treasure are gone, but the story lives like the
  leaves,
The story I told of our loves that was writ on the poets' staves.

XIII

'No youngster ever had so much to tell
Of all he sees when he is journey-bound,'
Said Croftnie the Harp-player to the lad,
As following Prince Leary's in their own
Chariot they sped.

'Croftnie, now I see
The twisting spokes and bronze rims of the wheels
That bear my father's chariot, and I see
The springing deer, the rising flocks of birds.
The men who guard the fords that we splash through
And guard the causeways have curved blades of bronze
On lengthy handles and wear leathern cloaks.
And now the forest with its heavy branches
And gorges where the rocks are shaped like dragons,
Where shouting boys are driving grunting swine.
The forest of itself makes other sound—
What is it, Croftnie, you that listen well?'

'The sound the acorns make in falling down—
A galloping sound.'

'What see you, Croftnie?'
'The change, I think, that's coming over all.
Your father's grandfather, Ugony the Great,
Had set a mould of custom round men's ways:
He lived so long that he
Had broken Change to be a household beast—
The wild-lynx Change went softly through the land:
Music greatly flourished
Since there were no debates to din it down,
No wars to clash it from the people's ears.

144

But long-lived Ugony the Great is dead:
Now Change will growl and snarl and tear flesh—
I see her widely opened wild-lynx eyes.'

'But now my father goes to take the rule.'

'He is a worthy Prince, none worthier
To set his feet upon the Stone of Kings,
But wide as to the Northern Islands where
The skylarks sing all night, the gap between
His time and Ugony's, if I know aught.'

'Where skylarks sing all night—was that as far
As where the ship had come from?' the lad asked,
Mentioning the ship that had come in from Gaul.
Its traffickers would come up to the fair
That was in memory of Tighernmas
Who back in ancient times first smelted gold,
And thereby gave us means to pay for metal,
And stuffs and wares, and have besides the craft
Of shaping gold: all this the Harper told him
As the chariots turned towards the fair.
Prince Leary would keep ancient custom up,
And figure at the fair before he went
To set his feet upon the Stone of Kings.

The beach was reached; above it was the green
Where the fair was, the games and the assembly—
The ship was to be seen.

                    That ship from Gaul!
It was not spoken of by Leary's son—
It was too strange to wonder at, too lone:
It sank into his memory as sinks
Into the water's depth an offering
Made to the guardian of an uncrossed lake.

Amber and jet the traffickers had brought
Up from the ship with other stuffs and wares,
And set their jet and amber by our bronze—
Trumpets and level swords; the ribs of gold
That are our riches were well eyed by them,
And the wrought gold which cerds* of ours who have
Chief supply have customed skill in shaping:
There were the thin gold crescents, and besides
A sunlike piece, ribbed, ridged, and whorled
That would be the chief treasure of a King
Whose realm was beyond Dunuvius River.

Croftnie made mention of the things of note
To Leary's son. 'Amber,' he said, 'is here—
These wedge-like pieces on a deer-skin laid:
Burnished by sunshine in a northern land,
The autumn leaves have colour like these pieces.'
'Now one speaks with my father,' said the lad,
'And I would listen to his strange-toned speech.'
'He is the chief of merchants,' Croftnie said.

'Iron is harder, and with iron, swords
Can be made longer by another reach,'
And these words answered Leary who had asked
How lengthier swords and harder could be made,
Seeing the merchant turn from the bronze.
'In Gaul and in Beyond-Gaul men have forged
Iron into swords, and with such weapons
New lands, rich treasures gain in east and south.
A leader of the Gauls
Got gold to weigh his sword and scabbard down
When a head-city, Rome,
Was taken by the Followers of Bran.'

'What makes he on the ground?' asked Leary's son.

* Cerd: *artificer*.

146

'The Sign of Bran,' said Croftnie, and the lad,
'I'll look upon the Sign.' But Croftnie said,
'The War-god Bran—back with him into Gaul,'
For he knew tribes that kept the name of Bran
Living upon the fringes of the realm
Ugony had ruled—great Ugony who was dead.

But now a man upon a coppery horse
Rode up beside the chariots and the guards.
'My father's name he shouts,' said Leary's son.

'The news he's brought sends us another way,'
Said Croftnie, 'we go through Cavach's lands,
Cavach, your father's brother who is dead
As told the messenger. The kin would have your father
Stand with the mourners by Prince Cavach's bier.'

'The twisting spokes and bronze rims of the wheels
That bear my father's chariot I see,
With guards beside it running with their spears
Held lengthwise and their cloaks of otter-skin.
What see you, Croftnie, in this open land?'

'The Gaul your father spoke with talked of iron
In use beyond the sea. A prophecy
May be fulfilled: it is that when men use
A dark, dense metal Change will surely come.'

'But that is far away. Will what I look on
Be different? Look, Croftnie—
Geese gather in a hollow and smoke rises
Through roofs of wattled houses; sparks are blowing
Out of a cerd's house, and a woman's milling
Her grain in a stone's hollow with a stone—
Croftnie, will these things change?'

'I do not know:
But long-lived Ugony the Great is dead:
Here are Prince Cavach's cattle with their herdsman;
I know the mark that's on them. There's the mound:
And there's Prince Cavach's house upon the mound.
Your uncle will not take you on his knee.'

'Croftnie, I know. He will not, being dead.'

'And will be buried in the ancient way
As told the messenger—you will see it so.
Cavach, the crafty brother, is no more.
He might have edged a place too close to him
Who'll set his feet upon the Stone of Kings.'

Below the mound on which was Cavach's house
An unyoked chariot was placed for burial.
The man upon the coppery horse dismounted,
And bent his knee to what was in the chariot,
A stiff and swathed figure, and went away,
Drawing the guards who were with Leary's chariot.

Lifting his head to sniff to where they came,
Leaping the shafts, rubbing against the wheels,
A tame wolf ranged; beside the chariot
No people stood, and Leary's son looked on
Only the creature in which tameness strove
With wildness: then he saw his father cross
The sward and stand near where the wood-dog strained.

The figure that was stiff upon the chariot
Raised itself, a spear was in those hands.
And the lad saw the figure thrust the spear:
His father fell
First on his knee, and then the figure, standing
Upon the chariot, drove the spear down through him.
The body lay
Like a cut tree; the spear-wielder sprang down.

He heard a whisper:
'Leary is dead; Cavach, his brother killed him;
They've cut our guards off from us; we'll not live.'
And then he ran to where his father lay,
And thence was dragged to face a dark-faced man
Who stood beneath a tree with men about him,
His followers who held long, ready spears.

And he was helpless there—not even the words
He formed to fling into that face would come;
Only his breath he heard; he knew he'd lost
The use of speech; he formed the words again:
'Maen,' 'Speechless' was the word they used of him.
'Your father's in the burial-chariot now;
I'll be the one to follow the old King,
And turn the Kingship into mine own line.'
The lad would speak; he tried once more and could not,
And heard himself named 'Maen' by those about.

Then Cavach said, 'There is no need to slay
A speechless one. Never can he dispute
The Kingship with me nor those born of me.'
'You'll let Maen live?' asked Harper Croftnie.
'I'll let him live,' said Cavach, 'take him hence—
Not to his father's, for that house goes down,
But where you will.' Then Croftnie took him up
And carried him; he held a body stiffened
Against his own, and went forsaken paths.

   They went far that day
And reached a mark famous for sight and sound—
A waterfall with a cromlech nigh it:
There Croftnie the Harper set him down—
The lad who had no name but what was flung him—
Under the cromlech of a King whose name
Was lost before great Ugony's was heard of.

And the rain washed from the stones and streamed
To where the river swelled; the trees were black,
And there was nothing for a man to look at
In all the land but the wide face of the rain.

XIV

'BELOW there are white-faced throngs,
Their march is a tide coming nigher;
Below there are white-faced throngs,
Their faith is a banner flung higher;
Below there are white-faced throngs,
White swords they have yet, but red songs;
Place and lot they have lost—hear you not?
For a dream you once dreamed and forgot!'

'But a dream has a life of its own—
The wizard seas it can cross—
A dream has a life of its own—
It comes like the albatross.
A dream has a life of its own,
From my feet to your feet it has flown—
And you, you victorious
That wild, white thing will lose!'